The 2 Hour Garden

The 2 Hour Garden

Edited by Roger Grounds
Consultant Editor George Elbert

DOUBLEDAY & COMPANY, INC.
Garden City, New York

Copyright © 1976 by Times Newspapers Limited
All Rights Reserved
Printed in the United States of America
First Edition in the United States of America
First Published in Great Britain by Ward Lock Limited

Contents

6	Foreword	78	Stage 24: *Propagation and other skills*
		80	Stage 25: *Getting to know your garden*
9	**Part One**: From Start to Garden	82	Stage 26: *More plants/more ideas*
10	The Challenge	84	12 Months in
12	The First 6 Months	86	Recap of Workplans 14–26
14	Workplans 1–13	87	The Trial Gardens
16	The Second 6 Months		
18	Workplans 14–26	91	**Part Two**: The Gardens
20	The Trial Gardens	92	Branching Out on Your Own
24	Tools of the Trade	94	The Ornamental Garden
26	Stage 1: *High-speed screens/cheating the weather*	96	The Miniature Garden
28	Stage 2: *Getting the colour moving*	98	The Paved Garden
30	Stage 3: *Cover vines/starting tomatoes*	100	The Town and Roof Garden
32	Stage 4: *Starting marrows/squashes and sunflowers*	102	The Historical Garden
34	Stage 5: *Improving the lawn/using perennials*	104	The Secret Garden
36	Stage 6: *Starting the patio*	106	The Hanging Garden
38	Stage 7: *Finishing the patio + the herb garden*	108	The Damp and Shady Garden
40	Stage 8: *Changing the lawn shape*	110	The Invalid Garden
42	Stage 9: *Of gladioli/dahlias and perfect lawns*	112	The Indoor Garden
44	Stage 10: *Edging the lawn/plant types*	114	The Conservatory Garden
46	Stage 11: *The cottage garden/perennial patch*	116	The Bulb Garden
48	Stage 12: *Colchicums/seeding a lawn*	118	The Everlasting Garden
50	Stage 13: *Trees are forever*	120	The Rose Garden
52	6 Months in	122	The Perfumed Garden
54	Recap of workplans 1–13	124	The Herb Garden
55	The Trial Gardens	126	The Vegetable Garden
58	Stage 14: *Bulbs large and small*	128	The Fruit Garden
60	Stage 15: *Erecting a trellis/planting vines*	130	The Seaside Garden
62	Stage 16: *All about soil*	132	The Ecological Garden
64	Stage 17: *A fruit tree/a sunny wall/improving soil*	134	The Future Garden
66	Stage 18: *Choosing shrubs/rockery/rock garden work*		
68	Stage 19: *Herbaceous perennials/bug hunting*	136	Summary
70	Stage 20: *Planting containers/soil testing*	137	Bug Recognition Chart
72	Stage 21: *Ivy tubs and a living fly repellent*	139	Glossary of Gardening Terms
74	Stage 22: *House plants/cuttings*	140	Glossary of Latin and Common Names
76	Stage 23: *The art of pruning*	142	Index

Foreword

As our urban areas spread further and further, and gardening plots are squeezed to small back yards or patios, the problems of modern horticulture have switched from large to small scale planning. Much of the original plot layout and building has been done and the new generation faces the task, when buying or renting a home in city or suburb, of turning many a yard, neglected by previous owners, into an attractive and productive environment for modern plant lovers.

Faced with this situation we have recourse to books and there we find any number of no doubt clever ideas of how a finished garden should look. Alas, the question remains: how do we begin? And then – since we have no previous experience: What are the succeeding steps? What do we buy and what do we sow? How much work is involved?

Well, of course, no book can supply definitive answers because every situation is different. A set of procedures and work periods perfectly suited to a family in Scotland or Maine will be quite different from those for a Devonshire or Virginia gardener. But we are all obliged to adjust rules to particular circumstances, and this is true of gardening as of everything else. Otherwise it would be impossible to benefit from the experience of others. That being the case, all that was required in the small renovation and revival gardening field was a book which would lead the beginner by the hand, as it were, from step to step. And, if all the necessities were included, it would be useful to anyone with that kind of problem.

Well, this is that book. And the authors have been most clever and inventive in grappling with the thirst for information. For, instead of concentrating on one imaginary garden, several real families and garden renovation situations were chosen. Each one had a different plan to work with, but the elements in each instance were the same. The work period was arbitrarily fixed at an average of 2 hours a week and the question raised and tested – How much of the planned garden could be accomplished within the time quota?

Well, it didn't work out perfectly – and it was impossible that it should—since people and situations are so different. But the most skilful and hardest worker in the group did manage to make an almost miraculous transformation. That proved at least the possibilities. And the whole enterprise did show that, by adjusting your own pace to your needs, a remarkable amount of creative gardening work can be accomplished with relatively little time spent on it. Let us say that 2 hours is not enough for you. You can divide it up differently or work a little longer. But at least here are all the elements, the ideas, the materials and the plants.

And then, having established the basic garden, a series of imaginative continuations are presented – ones that challenge but do not bind – wildly suggestive to stir up your own dreams of the perfect garden.

Here is a book which meets a modern need and supplies the answers.

Good Gardening.

George Elbert

Part One

From Start to Garden

The Challenge

The problem: confined space (25 ft. × 30 ft.), a town environment, poor soil on a clay base, an ugly shed, a rough lawn, an open-paling fence and a slatted fence giving inadequate privacy – a blank brick wall, obtrusive paths, a tree beneath which little grows, an uninviting overall design plan.

Does your back garden look something like this? Has lack of time, money and, perhaps, enthusiasm, prevented you from tackling it? If so, this book is for you. It is aimed primarily at the first-time gardener who would like his yard to look better but has so far shrunk from the problems he/she imagines are involved. And it offers adventurous new ideas for the experienced gardener as well. Half the guide concentrates on one particular situation, the small urban garden (right) whose challenges we have concentrated into one 'indentikit' problem garden and for which we have devised a fortnightly series of simple work projects that can be adapted – and have been tested – in a wide variety of different

gardens. These projects involve an average expenditure of two hours work per week (more in the summer, of course, and less in the winter) a minimal cash expenditure and create in 6 months a riot of colour, and in 12 a garden whose future maintenance should consume a minimum of time and money. The planting programme is restricted to sturdy plants which have a better chance than most of withstanding the worst that poor soil, town air – and inexpert gardeners – can do to them.

You can take or leave any part without leaving your garden looking like a battlefield. And the programme is also designed to teach most of the basic gardening skills and techniques. The other half of the guide provides a kaleidoscope of suggestions for all sorts of specialist gardens, gardeners and garden users: new ways with lilies, bulbs and roses; how to provide pleasure in the garden for invalids, children or even pets and sports enthusiasts; cottage/perennial, roof, rock and water gardens; the latest ideas in garden decoration, lighting and design, indoors and out; using vegetables and fruit as ornamentation – like, say, the strawberries illustrated (bottom); how to encourage and protect wild life by, for example, planting a buddleia that will attract butterflies.

These projects have been devised for the more experienced gardener who already has an established garden, possibly in a rural or suburban setting. But many of the ideas are applicable to the humblest town yard or cabbage patch, and both parts of our book share the same basic principles: to put life back into the soil as the basis for exciting plant life; to work ecologically wherever possible, avoiding poisons, encouraging wild life and recycling waste; and, above all, to make the garden a place that is fun both to work and relax in.

The First 6 Months

In just 6 months the ratty tatty almost barren backyard shown on page 10 could look as pretty and productive as this.

You don't believe it? Maybe you're thinking along conventional gardening lines. Suspend your disbelief for a while.

Your first problem is tired soil. Your plot will have been subjected to a continuous rain of soot – which will have made the soil too acid to grow much that is worthwhile – and to the dirt from the fumes of internal combustion engines – mainly lead – which will have killed off much of the life in the soil itself. The nearest thing to fertilizing the soil will have been done by the usual array of local stray cats. Furthermore, from sheer lack of attention your soil will have become so compacted that drainage is non-existent. All of which means that your soil will be too acid, too infertile and too compacted to grow anything other than the most pernicious and persistent of weeds. If the previous owners of your property were of the non-gardening sort, chances are that you will find just below the top couple of inches of soil a curious array of miscellaneous rejected building materials – bricks, tiles, concrete lumps and so on deposited there during building. There's nothing there to get the plants growing.

We start revitalizing the soil by feeding it with moss peat, because it's easy to buy. Later we'll put compost on it – compost we make ourselves in the garden. We'll tell you how. But starting that compost bin for later use is one of the first things to do.

Then we start a crash programme to get quick-growing foliage cover and colour into the garden. Take a colour shot of your garden as it is now, so you can compare it with later snaps as work progresses.

Flip over to pages 14/15. On page 15 there is a plan of a garden, and a view of the garden seen from the house. Relate the numbers on the plan to the numbers in the view – then look up the number in the text to find what it represents. The plan is designed to be adaptable to almost any small garden. If it's very long and thin, simply double the plan, dividing the two with a hedge or screen with an arch in the middle. Draw your own plan in rough: then colour key it into the master plan as shown here. Keep the colours the same, the numbers the same. Each number/colour is the major project of one of the 13 fortnights in the first 6 months in your garden. Stick to the same number/colour coding and you'll have a garden as pretty and productive as this at the end of stage 13.

Workplans 1-13

1. **A bean bed** can provide not only fresh vegetables for the kitchen – three crops in the case of our particular garden, broad, French and runner – but also put life back into worn soil by assisting nitrogen fixation while creating dense, rapid-growing foliage cover along a fence.
2. **The annual bed** should create a splash of 'instant colour' in the foreground of your garden. Later we list a selection of cheerful hardy annuals and explain how to plant the two illustrated here – the marigold and the Shirley poppy.
3. **Covering vines** provide the solution to bare walls and such eyesores as bomb-shelters, boiler-houses and oil central-heating tanks. Our third instalment shows how to plant convolvulus and ornamental hop – two really fast vines.
4. **Our summer display bed** sports one annual, the sunflower, and a popular perennial, the butterfly gladiolus, a corm. We shall list alternatives – the sunflower performs best against a warm sheltered wall; we have selected the gladiolus to show how to plant, and later how to raise and propagate corms.
5. **Our autumn display bed** provides an opportunity to learn about, and how to care for, different sorts of plant: a tuber, the dahlia and a root clump, the Korean chrysanthemum.
6. **The patio** is what people tend to call the patch of concrete outside their French windows. We think that sitting in the garden should be literally that – sitting *in* it, and so we show how to lay the base of our patio so that it breaks up the line of the path along the fence.
7. **Patio paving** is a heavy task, building on the preparation carried out before and seeking to blend the paved area and lawn.
8. **The lawn** *could* be left uncut. It would stand up better to children playing on it if left shaggy. But we have included a regular shave in our weekly timetable, and have altered its shape drastically – though not until the eighth instalment and 16th week; by then you should know if you want to go past the point of no return. The faint-hearted could just round their lawn edges into curves.
9. **Summer bedding plants,** in our case French marigolds and nasturtiums (nice in salads), are bought as young plants and planted to enliven odd dull corners and gladioli.
10. **Our vegetable patch** should be decorative as well as nourishing: lettuces, carrots, radishes and onions planted round a tropical-looking marrow or gourd.

11. **Our cottage/perennial garden corner** is a gesture at rusticity where tree roots make deep digging difficult: periwinkle running to the edge of the lawn, where thymes and sedums are planted between paving-stones the mower can run over.

12. **A compost heap** is the heart of a good garden, but if you have little space to play with, or byelaws limit you, you may decide to throw all your plant waste away and rely on artificial fertilizers.

13. **An ornamental tree** rounds off our first six months work. It is one of the few permanent fixtures in a planting programme designed to show how rapidly a barren garden can be rejuvenated during the spring and summer growing season. If left, much of this garden as it stands will die down through the autumn and winter and will need replanting again next year. Since our ultimate aim is a garden that will, on the whole, require little maintenance and replanting, we must now move on to consider the long-term strategy that will give our garden permanent shape.

The numbers and key colours on the plan (above) and tracing (left) refer to the components of the garden (right). Each chart will be discussed in detail during the growing season; the sequence will not be exactly the same as this diagrammatic order here.

The Second 6 Months

Next spring, after only 104 hours work spread over a total of 26 fortnightly projects your garden should look something like this.

Now if you think that this garden looks just a little less luxuriant than the one shown on pages 12/13 you just could be right. Because that picture shows your garden in high summer – just about the most colourful time of all in the garden – and it shows a garden stuffed with annuals – a group of plants that pack more flower-power punch than any others. For a true comparison flick back to the garden shown on page 10 – that's how your garden looked 12 months ago. Both show your garden at the same time of year.

From that standpoint the differences are substantial. It looks like a different garden. It seems somehow to have relaxed, to flow and harmonize, and more than that, it seems to invite you to go out into it and explore it. You never felt that way about the garden on page 8. Changing the shape of the lawn to a circle or near circle probably does more to make a garden feel relaxed than any other single thing. And with the garden feeling that much more relaxed, it's worth having the permanent features like the patio. After all, would you really have wanted to sit out in the garden shown on page 8?

With the permanent features you've created your garden is a joy to look at at any time of year. Its got shape and form. Now you've largely revitalized your soil, there are ground cover plants under that big old tree, and between that and your cottage garden/ perennial patch; there are shrubs and climbers that will flower later in the season, the plants in the containers on the patio, and in the foreground herbaceous perennials that will increase in size and flower power year by year. You'll get a lot more colour this year for a very great deal less work.

And your garden should run itself pretty much from now on, so long as you just check up on the groundwork. And so long as you keep using compost and/or moss peat to mulch/feed the ground and smother the weeds.

As before, the plan and view bottom right show the colour/ number key to the second 6 months main projects. Work them out on your own plan. Stick to the code.

Workplans 14-26

14. **Bulbs** provide the focus of spring colour: tulips in our former vegetable patch; daffodils and hyacinths where the annuals were; and bluebells in the patio pots. Our garden has been designed so that these areas provide displays of changing colour – bulbs in spring, annuals in summer and autumn – but gardeners wishing to avoid replanting could simply naturalise bulbs like crocuses in the lawn and permanent beds.

15. **Trellis** provides a framework to mask our shed and give privacy. This is quite an expensive investment and one of our winter tasks will be to put it up *securely* so that wind, cats and heavy plants cannot bring it down.

16. **Permanent ground-cover** – we select nepeta (catmint) from the possibilities we discuss. This occupies our former bean bed, and runs from the periwinkle planted in our cottage-garden corner to the rockery we shall site near our ornamental tree.

17. **Our living hedge** is a *Cotoneaster simonsii*, an evergreen wall of colour across the end of the garden. Its berries will attract birds, so gardeners with vegetables to protect may prefer to select one of the other varieties we shall suggest.

18. **The shrub bed** occupies the site of our summer display bed and has been designed as a corner that will be of year-round interest. A flowering quince and a rhododendron are shown here with their spring flowers. The evergreen mahonia will produce yellow flowers during the late winter and spring when the berberis and viburnum will also come into their own.

19. **The herbaceous border** is a bed of plants that will last for more than one season, most of them being perennial. In addition to the Korean chrysanthemums and dahlias planted earlier in the year, we shall transfer to this bed the butterfly gladioli corms and plant pyrethrum, scabious and coreopsis. Rather better results will be achieved if you take up and replant the roots every three or four years.

20. **Climbing roses** and *Clematis montana* provide permanent cover and delicate flowers on our trellis.

21. **A herb bed,** grown from seed indoors and transferred outside, provides an aromatic fringe to the patio.

22. **A fan espaliered tree** (any fruit tree whose branches are trained outwards to spread across a wall) can be bought ready trained. Correctly sited and planted it should yield good fruit.

23. **Decoration** can range from pebbles to marble cupids – our budget limits us to the former – scattered amid aubrietia and

alyssum round the base of our ornamental tree. Big spenders can, of course, take up any of the decorative ideas that will be featured in Part Two.

24. Our rockery/rock garden is a modest affair making use of earth excavated from our patio and tree-planting activities. But we shall show how to make dramatic use of rocks and plants, even on a small scale.

25. Container plants are the only type of vegetation that can enliven an increasingly common type of town garden – the paved or gravelled yard. Properly prepared, planted and watered, outdoor pot plants can yield exciting, colourful results and we suggest several varieties: balsams and begonias, trailing nepeta, lobelia, campanula, Canary creeper and, as a change from the upright variety, the ivy-leafed geranium that flops most enticingly.

26. Christmas-present plants need not go into the dustbin after Twelfth Night. Azaleas, hyacinths, winter cherry, and other gift plants can be brought out to enhance a patio or ornamental bed.

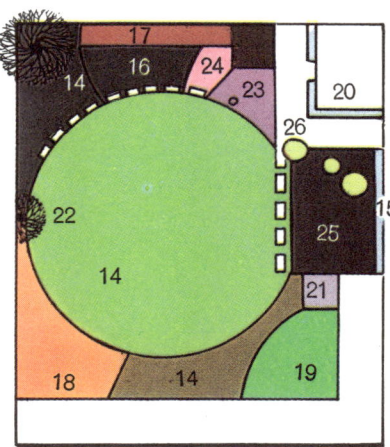

Where work projects in the second half of the gardening year are sited in areas that were planted during the earlier growing season, identical or similar colours are used for both periods. Thus bulbs are the same colour as the annuals were, and so on.

The Trial Gardens

On page 10 we showed you a picture of a typical weary, stale, flat and totally uninteresting and unamusing urban or suburban garden. There must be thousands like it up and down the UK and America. Then we showed you how it could be transformed in just 6 months into a riot of colour. And then how after 12 months and only 104 hours work it could be turned into a permanently delightful garden that would need little work to keep it as a joy for ever. We gave you perspective views of the garden at both 6 months and 12 month stages, and ground plans for both, colour coded and number keyed into the 26 workplans needed to achieve those results. We also claimed that you could adapt that basic ground plan to suit just about any urban or suburban garden, using all the workplans, or selecting those items you liked and rejecting those you didn't.

On the following pages we'll show how that basic plan can be adapted to suit 6 quite different gardens, owned by people with quite different needs. Pick the plan that is nearest the shape of your garden, and draw up your own garden plan based on that. Just make sure you keep to the same number/colour coding as we do or you may end up with results you never expected.

There's one very important point here. We didn't choose the gardens. The gardens came to us. We had to make the most of them, just as you will need to adapt the plan to suit your garden.

And with the gardens came the people who owned them. Gardens without people are nothing. Because gardens reflect the individuality of the people who own them, in just the same way as your sitting room reflects you whether you like it or not.

None of them was a dedicated gardener. None had particularly clear ideas of the sort of garden they wanted. They were all people who were happy to take our basic groundplan, and try it. From that point of view they started level with you. They did the same things in their gardens as you will, at the same time, following the same stages. But we'll be reporting on their progress after 6 months and at the end of a year. Measure your progress against theirs. You'll find you'll be better than some, and worse than others. Learn from their mistakes.

For a start, let's meet our 6 volunteer gardeners.

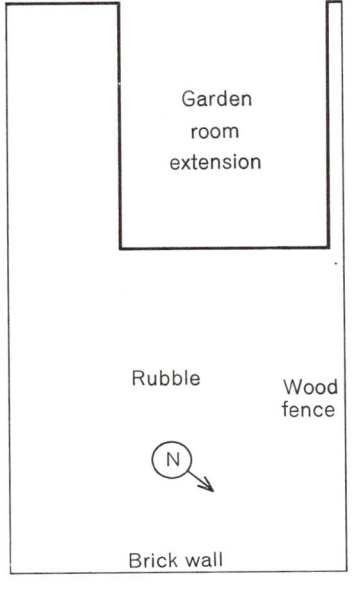
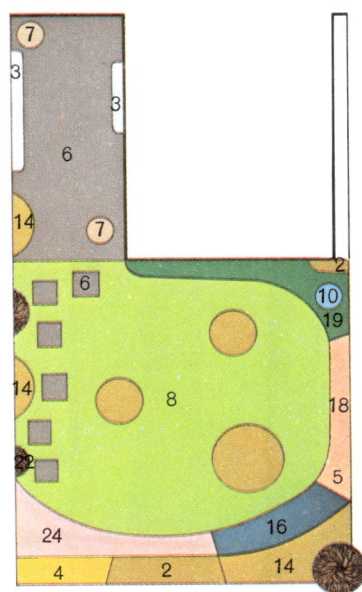

Michael and Angela Harding had just moved in to their new home. Their garden looked like a battlefield – full of builder's rubble – such a mess even weeds hadn't grown. By September, they hope their garden room extension will be complete. They planned to use their patio for eating and entertaining and to provide ropes, swings and a sandpit in the main area for their children, James (three) and Alexandra (one-and-a-half). The accent of their borders was planned to be on colourful flowers rather than on vegetables, but they may take up some of the more exotic suggestions in our specialist fruit and vegetable garden instalments. These, together with the problems caused by builders' rubble, will probably take them over the basic two-hour budget, but one elegant touch should be inexpensive: they plan to sling a hammock between two existing lilac trees.

Dr William James likened his all-walled, shaded garden to a prison yard. The sun only reaches the very lightest part of it for three months of the year, and then for a maximum of two hours per day. At this stage it was a wilderness of weeds, mainly grasses, with a few abandoned paving stones lying around. Since he has to look out at it from his kitchen window he wanted to improve the view, and was also attracted by the prospect of harvesting his own fruit and vegetables. He felt little enthusiasm for a lawn since he was keen to provide cover for birds, whose diversity in central London fascinates him. He tested the flexibility of our timetable with the toughest challenge of all: he took time off to cycle over the Andes.

Kenneth and Heather MacLeod started with the most established of the gardens in which our year-long series of work projects was tested. They intended to use the components of our workplans to soften the formality of the backyard that was already trellised when they bought their home three years ago. Heather said 'We would like our garden to be a safe place for our baby son Alexander to play in, an outdoor room where we can sit and relax, and also the starting-point of a new and creative hobby.' You'll note that they've dropped several components, but they've rounded most of the corners in their 4-square garden and used paved areas both sides of their trellis division, reversing the plan top to bottom from one half of the garden to the other.

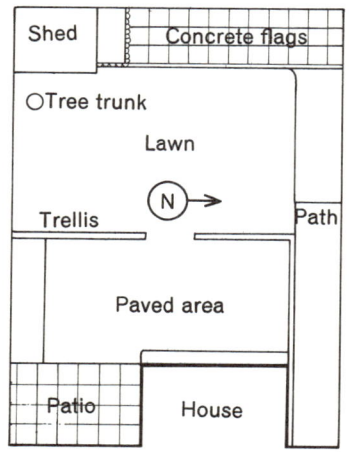
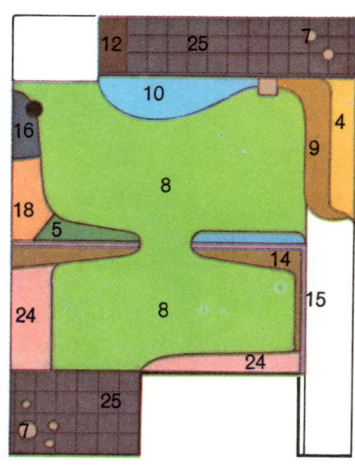

John and Janey Allan's garden is twice as large as any of the other volunteer gardens. They planned to split it in two, the half nearest the house resembling the base plan shown in this book, the rear half becoming a cultivated area to supply fresh fruit and vegetables for Janey's deep freeze cookery business. At this stage the garden was all weeds, 1 apple tree and 1 dilapidated garden shed. One complication was couch grass which had grown over all the paths and beds. The only way to eradicate this is to dig up the roots and burn them, and rather than go over the entire 67 ft. × 27 ft. area with a spade, John Allan planned to get the job done with a hired Rotavator/rotatiller (a powered digging machine). The Allans expected to use their patio for entertaining and their garden as a play area for their baby daughter Sophie.

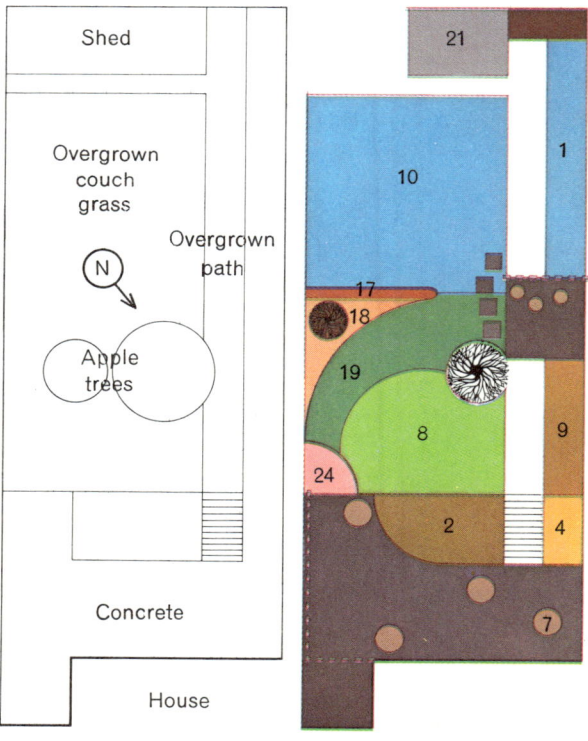

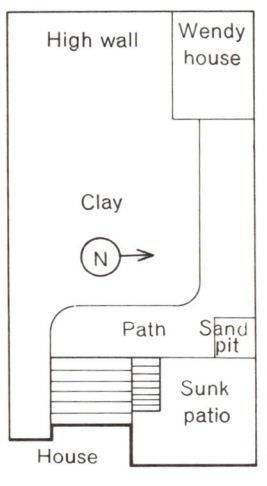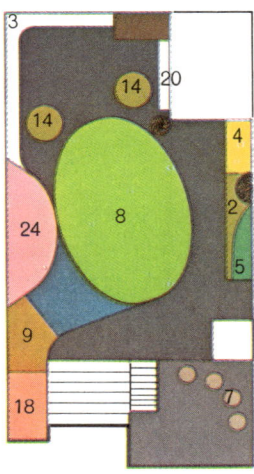

Solid clay was the problem in the garden of Timothy and Penelope Hicks. So they aimed to shift some of it to provide a basis for their rockery/rock garden, and bring in six cubic yards of topsoil to give a foot depth to their flower-beds and lawn. This could cost quite a lot, but once they had created average garden conditions they hoped to be able to keep within our basic needs list. Their patio splits their garden into two levels – the lower one for sunbathing and entertaining. This change of level adds immediate and dramatic effect to an otherwise small and drab town garden. The upper level has a swing and sandpit for Sophia (seven), Edward (five) and Oliver (one-and-a-half), and a kid's playhouse where Matthew (nine) has slept out. Timothy Hicks was keen to cover the walls around his garden with vines and climbing roses.

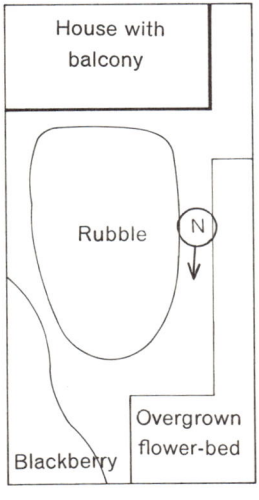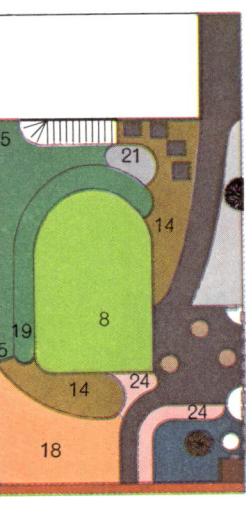

Michael and Jackie Thorpe had been renovating their new home for over a year before starting on the garden. 'It's our first, so we want to keep it fairly fluid. We may change the design as we go along,' said Michael Thorpe. 'It must be tough enough for the kids and for the dog as well. We want the sort of plants that will encourage the birds to visit.' He hoped to build a climbing frame on the lawn for his son Lucas (four) and, later, his daughter Polly (six months) to play on, and planned to concentrate on flowers rather than vegetables to give full colour to the borders. His ultimate aim was a garden involving as little work as possible. At this stage the garden looked like a demolition man's yard, full of rubble from the renovations.

Tools of the Trade

There's an old old saw that it's a bad workman who blames his tools. That really isn't fair on the workman, or the tools. You just simply would not expect the plumber to do a good job if his only tools were a needle, thread and scissors, any more than you would expect your tailor to do a good job if his only tools were a spanner and blowlamp. So don't expect to do a good job in your garden if you only arm yourself with a teaspoon and a buckled fork.

There are two ways of looking at buying gardening tools. You can either buy just sufficient tools to do the job – or you buy tools specifically to impress the people next door. If you want to do that, just go to your garden centre and buy every manual, mechanical and electrical tool, device or gadget you can find. You'll never use three-quarters of them.

The tool kit we show is a basic tool kit, designed to do a basic job. Basic the kit may be, but there're enough tools there to see you through all your gardening needs for the next forty years. The important thing is to pay prices in the higher rather than the cheaper range, and to buy tools that feel right to you.

Here's a run-down on the tools you need. 1 Garden shears, for trimming new grass, clipping hedges. 2 Watering can – for watering almost everything. 3 Lawn mower – for mowing grass. 4 Dibbler, for planting seeds and marking lines. 5 Pruning shears/secateurs – for trimming plants. 6 Trowel, for taking out small holes in the ground for planting purposes. 7 Spade, for all basic digging. 8 Fork, for lighter digging, turning compost and so on. 9 Hoe, for keeping weeds down. 10 Rake, for working the surface of soil into a fine seedbed, removing stones and so on. Plus one good general gardening manual.

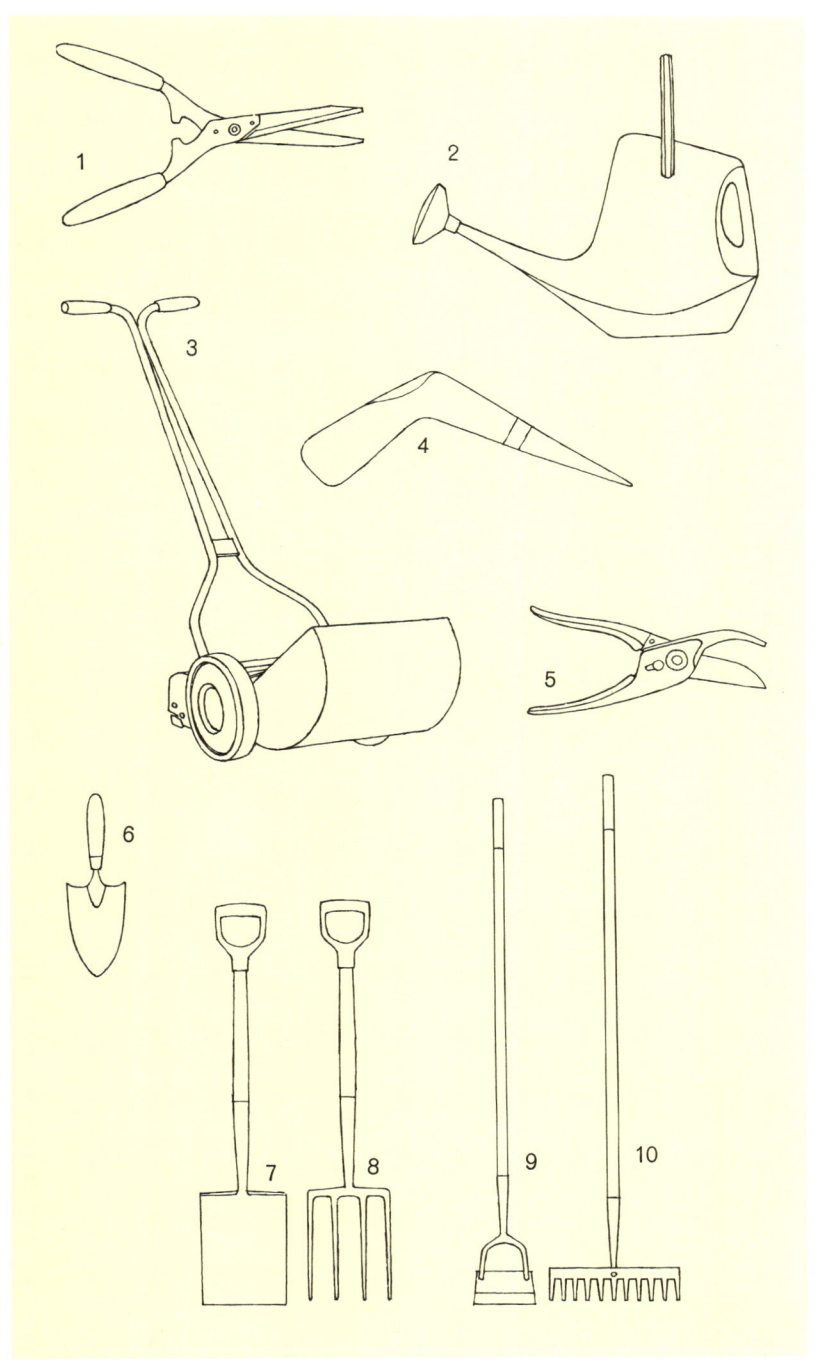

Stage 1

Worn soil and a bare open fence are the first challenges to be faced in our problem garden. The simplest way to beat them is by planting a fast-growing vegetable that provides an almost instant screen and which also puts some life into tired soil. Then we 'cheat' the weather by sowing seeds in pots indoors to keep them safe from late malicious frosts. And we build a compost bin to start our long-term soil rejuvenation programme.

Needs list: *1 pkt pole bean seeds; 1 bundle stakes or canes; 48 3 in diameter peat pots; ½ cwt/50 lb bag moss peat; 30 split larch poles.*
Time budget: *5 hours in 2 weeks*

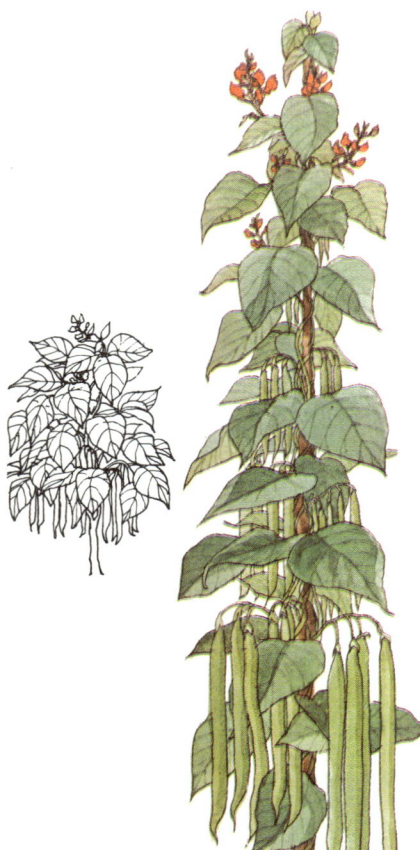

Flower of the Fortnight
Our first flower of the fortnight provides – in passing – a simple lesson in the value of Latin names. The English call this plant a scarlet runner bean. The Americans call it a scarlet runner. The English grow it for its long, edible beans, scarcely noticing its red or white flowers. The Americans grow it purely as an ornamental, for its scarlet flowers, considering the beans curious, but definitely not edible. The only way you know they're the same is their Latin name, *Phaseolus coccineus*. Either way, for food or flower, this is a high-speed annual vine, ideal for covering a fence fastest, and improving your soil while it does it. Grow dwarf French or bush snap beans in front to improve the soil there.

Groundwork
1 Every garden has stones. Where there's a stone there could be soil, a root, a plant. Pick out larger stones. Stack them in a corner or an old bin with holes in the bottom. Use later for drainage or for hard core. 2 Wood waste – shrub prunings or hedge clippings, woody root waste won't rot in the compost bin. Either burn them and use the sifted bonfire ash later to feed and level the lawn or add the ash to the compost heap; or dump them on your local tip. 3 Build yourself a compost bin. Forget compost heaps – they look untidy and don't compost waste properly. Build or buy a bin. Lots of good modern designs available from your local garden centre. Or build your own. Ours is a three-sided enclosure of bean posts from a wood yard, driven into the earth, enclosing the end of a path to save soil space. Ordinary wooden fence slats could be used. Throw any **vegetable** waste from garden or kitchen into the bin: *not* animal waste.

Early April weather/soil
Statistically winter is over by now and spring's on the wing if not actually arrived. Air temperature is rising, and the soil is getting warmer and drier. Plants are starting into growth. Time too, for humans to move outdoors, start gardening. Beware however of killing snap frosts.

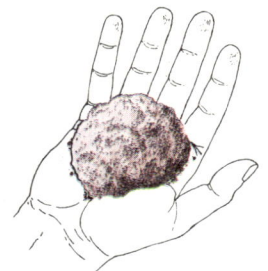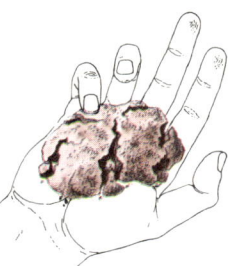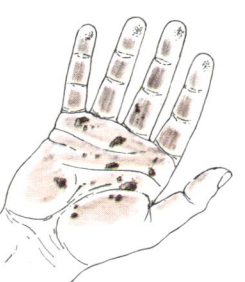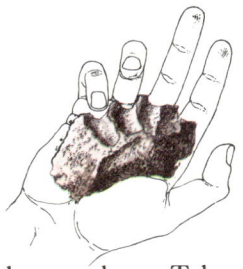

Project work: preparing and planting a pole bean

When to dig. One of the first things you will need to learn to do is dig.

You can't do much about creating a garden till you do. But how do you know when to dig: if the soil's too wet, it's back-breaking work: it's almost as difficult if it's too dry.

Here's how you know. Take a handful of soil. Compress it into a ball. It should be dry enough to break up when squeezed in the hand. When dropped it should leave a slight stain and some particles on your hand. O.K., start digging. If it coagulates in your hand wait till it's drier.

How to dig. Stand over your spade or fork. Direct your effort downwards through your shoulders. Bending your spine (the way most people dig) will only give you backache. It could actually damage your back. Dig to the depth of one spade or fork blade.

How to Plant. First of all prepare the bed in the garden. Dig it over thoroughly, picking out stones and roots. Then sprinkle 1 in. moss peat over the bed: that's at the rate of 7 lb/yd². Rake it in to form a rich easily worked soil. Move indoors and fill your peat pots loosely with a soilless growing mix. Do not compress it. Soilless mixes are meant to have a light, open texture. Push 1 bean seed 2 in. deep into each pot. Plant pots 9 in. apart in rows 18 in. apart. Water lightly. Keep 3 pots indoors to replace seed failures.

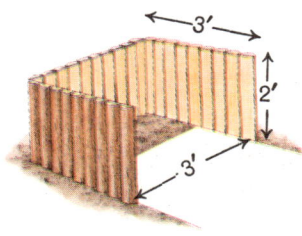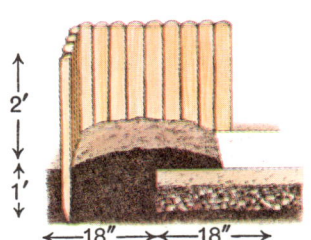

Stage 2

A fortnight ago we were sober and practical, planting a high-speed vine-type vegetable to hide us from our neighbours and improve the soil. Spring weather has made us more fun-loving. This time we're going for the boldest brightest splash of colour you ever saw in a garden right in the very front of the garden. All provided by two hardy annuals. Calendulas and Shirley poppies. With the first we sow the seeds individually: with the poppies we scatter them broadcast.

Needs list: *1 pkt Calendula seed – preferably pelleted; 1 pkt Shirley poppy seed; ½ cwt/50 lb bag moss peat; 1 pkt bonemeal.*
Time budget: *4 hours in 2 weeks*

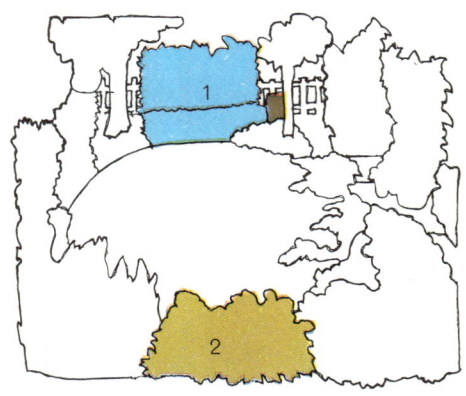

Flower of the Fortnight

The Shirley poppy belongs here because now's the time to sow the seed. In the warmer parts of the country you'll find it shoots up into flower so fast you may have your own seedlings in flower before fall. If not, save seed to sow again next year, for this is one of the easiest of annuals – one of those flowers no garden should ever be without. Collecting seed is easy: just tap the seedheads so the seeds fall into an envelope. Keep dry over winter. Plants look best near the back of a border, to show off the flowers in front. Though beautiful in themselves, their greatest garden value is that they help make other plants look even more exciting. Grows to 2 ft. tall. Flowers June till September.

Groundwork

1 Continue picking stones out of the soil. Stack or store as before for future use. 2 Continue burning wood waste. Save ash for future use. 3 Put all vegetable waste from home and garden into your compost bin. 4 If you already have a lawn and intend to mow it, make sure your mower is oiled and that the blades are sharpened ready for cutting. 5 Mark existing plants in your garden that you may wish to keep. Do this with a stick beside the plant. Signs of life should be appearing all over the garden now, so make the decision on what to keep and what to throw out now, before the greenery becomes too lush and dense. Then, with all the plants you want to keep safely marked with sticks, as markers, you can safely pull up any stray greenery that appears. 6 If the weather has been very dry, make sure that the soil in the peat pots planted in the bean bed (Stage 1) are kept moist but never wet at all times. Check all pots for signs of life. Whip out any pot that has not produced seedlings after 15 days, replace with reserve plants germinated indoors. Plant as before.

Mid April weather/soil

An unpredictable season this, raising hopes of summer to come with clear blue skies then dashing them with bouts of late frosts. Weather typically showery, blustery, given to sudden dry spells (hard on new-sprouted seedlings). Avoid the temptation to plant tender subjects yet.

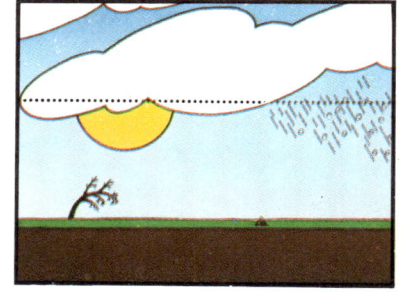

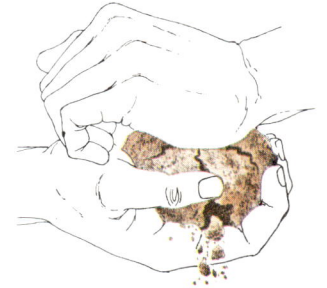

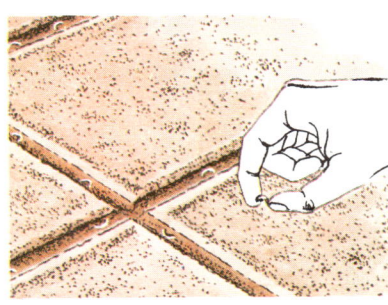
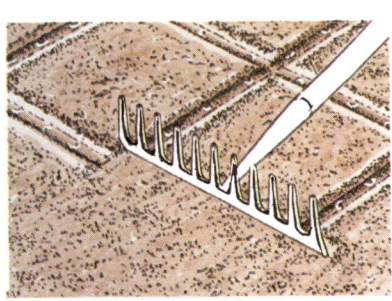
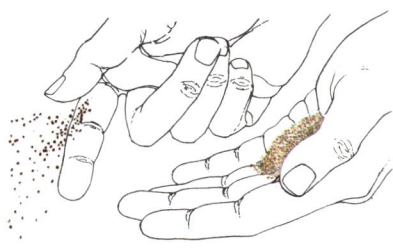
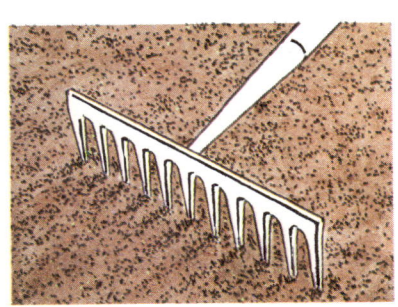

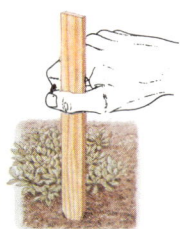

Project work: planting an annual bed with 2 colourful flowers

Dig over the entire bed as shown in Stage 1. Dig to a full 1 spit depth/a spade's depth, turning the soil thoroughly. Sort out all the larger stones and any roots, especially the white, thread like roots of pernicious perennial weeds such as couch grass, bindweed, ground elder. All these weeds will romp away if you leave so much as $\frac{1}{2}$ in. of root in the ground. Cover the soil with 1 in. moss peat = 7 lb./yd^2. Use double this quantity if your soil is very heavy clay or exceedingly fine sand. Using a garden fork, work the peat thoroughly into the top 6 in. of soil. Then sprinkle a top dressing of bonemeal over the bed; apply at the rate of 4 oz./yd^2. If you don't know what a yd^2 looks like, lay strings at 3 ft. intervals along one side of the bed, then more string at 3 ft. intervals at right angles to the first lot and over them. Apply 4 oz. in each square thus created. Next, make a criss-cross pattern at the front of the bed, using a dibbler or a stick. It's just like drawing patterns in the sand. What you want are criss-crossing straight lines, each $\frac{1}{2}$ in. deep with raised sides. Plant your calendula seeds individually 3–4 in. apart. The aim is not a regular pattern but a seemingly random array of flowers. This way you sow the seed right, and the end result looks just great. Cover the calendula seeds by drawing the soil back over them with the back of the rake. Take a handful of poppy seeds and broadcast them – just sprinkling them loosely over the soil with your fingers. Do this at the back of the bed behind the calendulas. These poppies, too, will come up in a dense, random fashion. Rake over the poppy seed lightly, so that they are buried in no more than $\frac{1}{8}$ in. Plant a few seeds of each in peat pots indoors. Use later as replacements where any patches of seed fail to come up. You should be able to tell by then.

Stage 3

Two major objectives to be accomplished this fortnight. First, it's time to cover-up unsightly walls, fences, sheds, concrete garages and central-heating oil-tanks. Such things can mar even the greenest of gardens. We'll show you how to plant some high-speed ornamental vines using a modern innovation – a presown tape dispenser. Second, it's time to get your tomato transplants into the ground. Every day you delay lessens your chance of a good crop.

Needs list: *1 pkt ornamental hop seed; 1 pkt convolvulus seed; 1 presown tape dispenser; 12 3 in diameter peat pots; 1 length 18 × 6 ft five in bean netting/chicken wire/trellis; 5 rustic poles 7–8 ft long; 1 ball garden twine; 1 pkt wire staples; 4–6 tomato transplants + tomato growing mix + liquid feed + tomato bag; one 2 pint garden sprayer.*
Time budget: *4 hours in 2 weeks*

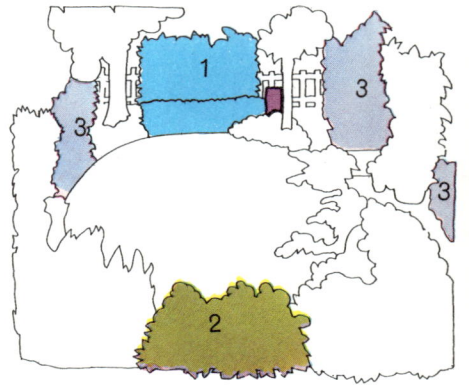

Flower of the Fortnight
If you've never grown a tomato before, start now. It's by far the most popular home gardener vegetable of all. Something like 8 times as many people grow tomatoes as any other vegetable. If you're going to grow them at all, set out to grow them better than anyone else in your street. They're not the easiest; success starts with starting the seed early. Plant out as soon as you dare, but don't risk frosting young plants. Then just keep watering and feeding (liquid feed) and praying for sun. There are bush and pole varieties – some of the bush ones are small enough for pots on the kitchen windowsill. Choose disease resistant varieties, and check catalogues for best varieties for your area.

Groundwork
1 Keep up the good work of collecting stones, stacking or storing them, and keep on adding vegetable waste to the compost bin. 2 Start mowing the lawn as soon as it starts into growth. Set the blades high for the first trim of the season. Just give it a light trim over the top. Lower the blades for a finer trim later in the season. 3 Examine vegetation (especially the beans) for aphids. There are two types: 1 blackfly; if plants are infected, pour two teaspoonsfuls of liquid detergent into two pints of cold water in the bottle part of a pressure insect spray. Hold the spray close to the blackfly and spray lightly. Spray again one week later. The other aphid type is greenfly – which looks just like the blackfly but is green. Problem is a green bug on a green stem is not always easy to spot – so examine vegetation very closely for this bug. Treat it the same way you treat blackfly. In both cases the bugs are killed because the solution clogs their breathing pores.

Early May weather/soil
May heralds true summer at last. Whatever the vagaries of earlier spring, weather and soil both warm up now and plant growth accelerates noticeably. So, too, does the rate of increase of garden bugs. Traditionally a dry month, this can be a problem, especially if rainfall was low earlier.

Project work: planting cover vines; using presown tapes; starting tomato transplants

First for the vines = Flower of the Fortnight, Stage 6. Prepare the bed as in Stage 1, digging out deep-rooting, pernicious, persistent weeds. Mix in moss peat as suggested in Stage 2. Top dress with bonemeal. Using peat pots again, filled with soilless growing mix, sow 3 seeds per pot. Plunge the pots in the ground under a warm wall to get the seeds off to a good start. Put a slanting pane of glass over the pots if late frosts or heavy rains threaten. Alternatively make a clear plastic sheeting tent (see illustration). When seedlings are 2 in. high, thin out the weakest two. 2 days later move peat pots to final positions, 4 in. in front of fence or trellis, spaced 12 in. apart. Use staples to fix mesh or trellis to mortar or to support poles in open ground at 4 ft. intervals. Tie in beans with twine or raffia. Alternatively sow seed in position using a presown tape and thin to 12 in. apart. Now for your tomatoes. Don't waste time starting from seed. Save that till you've more experience. Buy transplants from your garden centre. Choose plants with stems the thickness of a pencil. Avoid drawn, leggy seedlings or plants showing yellowing of the leaf. In the US and in virgin soil grow tomatoes in the ground. Take out a hole 12 in. deep, 18 in. across, refill with a mix of 50/50 nitrogen-rich compost and soil. After 2 weeks stake. Tie in plants as they grow. When they reach the top of the stake (about 4 ft.) pinch out the top. In the UK grow in tomato bags (ask your garden centre) or use ring culture. With tomato bags make an X-shaped slit and push your transplant through that into the growing mix inside the bag. For ring culture buy whalehide rings, stand them on a bed of ashes, fill with a tomato growing mix. Culture as for open ground plants. Always put tomatoes in the warmest place in your garden.

Stage 4

Time to add more colour to the garden, first with the giant-flowering sunflower, North America's biggest, brightest annual, widely grown for its nutritious seeds: eat your own crop or feed your pets when flowering's over. Time to get the marrows/squashes into the ground, delicious subtropical vegetables, but to succeed they need a little more loving than most. And definitely time to declare war on weeds; we tell you the options open to you: you choose.

Needs list: *1 pkt sunflower seed; 1 pre-sown pkt marrow/squash seed; 1 pkt 3 in diameter peat pots; ½ cwt/50 lb bag moss peat.*
Time budget: *4 hours in 2 weeks*

Flower of the Fortnight
America's mightiest contribution to the world of annual flowers is the annual sunflower, *Helianthus annuus*. This is a veritable jack-and-the-beanstalk plant, shooting up 10 or 12 ft. in six months, with large hairy leaves and a flower at the top at least the size of a dinner plate. Plant it at the foot of a south wall in a trench full of elephant manure, and you'll get it 15 ft. tall – no trouble. The world record is around 22 ft. Try that for size! For real garden effect you don't want them to get much over 5 ft., so plant them close – 18–24 in. apart. Your flowers will be as big, but the plants won't overpower everything else. Besides, they won't need staking. Plant 6 in in front of a wall.

Groundwork
War on weeds is essential if you are to cultivate your plot successfully. If they get a hold they'll crowd out the plants you want to grow. Life gets easier once your garden gets established. Concentrate on areas under cultivation; in large areas or areas you can't control effectively use ground cover plants or simply mow the weeds. Anyway – what is a weed? Useful definition – a plant out of place. Usually a wild plant that has invaded your plot. 3 ways you can deal with weeds. (1) hand weed (2) hoeing (3) chemical methods. 1 and 2 are to be preferred. Hand weeding is laborious but effective. Hoeing severs the growing top of the weed from its roots, forms green manure and a natural mulch of powdered soil. There are 3 types of weedkillers to choose from (1) total herbicides: these kill all plants in sight. (2) selective weedkillers – used mainly on lawns where they kill broadleaved plants like daisies, dandelions, but leave the grass growing. (3) pre-emergence weedkillers, which kill weed seeds before they come up. Use chemicals only as a last resort. If misused they kill people as well as weeds.

Mid May weather/soil
Weather dry, sunny: soil warm, workable. Take stock of the garden, now, before lush June masks the differences. Note where the favoured spots in the garden are, and where cold, damp soil or draughts retard growth. Avoid the cold, backward areas when deciding where to put the patio and tree.

Project work: starting marrows/squashes; getting the sunflowers growing

Your biggest task this fortnight will be to get your marrows/squashes/courgettes/pumpkins off to a good start. All are closely related: you grow them all the same way. Courgettes, in passing, are simply a type of marrow/squash that has been specially bred to pick very small. All marrows/squashes &c taste best if you pick them half to two-thirds the size the catalogues say they'll grow to. Don't wait till the outside feels like sunbaked rhino hide; by then they're inedible. Start by digging over an area of bare earth, clearing the weeds, stones, you know the drill by now. Then make a hill of compost or soilless growing mix 3 ft. across, about 1 ft.–18 in. high, hollowed in the centre. At the bottom of the hollow place half a bucketful of well-rotted farmyard manure or any other organic manure. Mix well. Top over with more soilless growing mix, still leaving a slight depression at the top of the hill. Plant 3 peat pots each with 2 marrow/squash seeds in them, pressing the pointed end into the growing mix. Thin out the weaker seedling of each pair 2 weeks later. Then plant the peat pots in the hills. Plant as close to the rim of the hill as you can, and plant the pots deeply, rims buried by about 1 in. Soak. Soak the hill weekly till you harvest. These plants need water. Mature marrows/squashes are 94·6% water, so it takes a lot of water to produce a crop. If you don't choose all female self-fertile marrows, you'll have to pollinate the flowers. Transfer pollen from male flowers (the ones with a cone in the middle) to the female flowers with a small paint brush. Or just push the male flowers into the female ones. If you don't pollinate, your marrows/squashes will be too bitter to eat. The plants are vigorous, sparwling things so allow them plenty of room. You'll get a head start if you start seeds indoors.

Stage 5

Three major items for this fortnight. First we plant the petunia, shown in the flower of the fortnight. Then we start on the herbaceous/perennial border. We'll plant a rootclump of Korean chrysanthemum. Then we add a Mexican beauty, the pom-pom dahlia Flower of the Fortnight, Stage 9. We plant tubers. They're frost tender so need to be lifted before frosts, stored dry over winter and replanted next spring. And we take a first look at the lawn.

Needs list: *6 petunia transplants; 7 dahlia tubers; 5 chrysanthemum plants; 1 pkt lawn food; 1 pkt bonemeal.*
Time budget: *4 hours in 2 weeks*

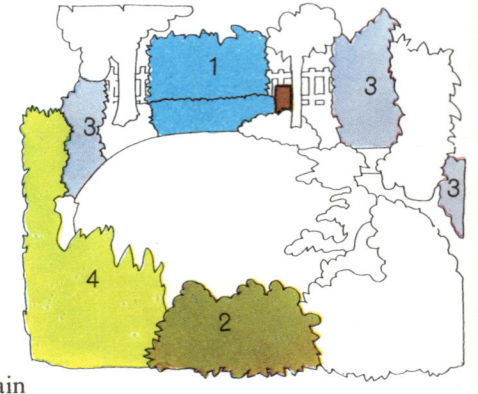

Flower of the Fortnight

Subtropical America is once again the native haunt of the flower of this fortnight – the petunia. Fantastically colourful flowers, with great, floppy trumpet-shaped blooms in almost every colour. Striped forms are probably the most effective: alternatively, plant clumps of white petunias among the coloured ones. Don't bother growing them from seed – you've enough other things to do anyway. Let the nurseryman grow them; just buy the transplants from him. Two tips for success: dig some bonfire ash into the soil before you plant. And when you plant, take out a hole with a trowel big enough to get all the roots in easily. Then firm and water. Give full sun, never let them dry out. Watch for slugs and other bugs.

Groundwork

By now the vegetable waste in your compost bin should be showing signs of decomposition. After every 6 in. of vegetable waste you put in, add a 1 in. layer of soil. If you're short of soil use moss peat, leaf-mould, farmyard manure, bonfire ash or – if you live out back of beyond – night soil. How do you know when you've laid down a 6 in. layer of waste? Paint red stripes on the back of the bin, each stripe 1 in. thick, 6 in. apart. The compost should never be allowed to become too wet or too hot. Beat winter wet and heavy storms by putting heavy-gauge plastic sheeting over the top. On the other hand, never let the heap dry out. In dry, hot weather, sprinkle lightly with the hose on it. Keeping the temperature right can be a problem. Fanatics take the temperature of their compost. Your nose is just as good a guide. If the heap smells like ammonia it's too hot: lift the waste with a fork to let air in to cool it. If it smells like a garbage dump it's too cool. Add an activator: urine is free and effective. Never put plants that have been weed-killed in the bin.

Early June weather/soil

June brings the longest days of the year to the northern hemisphere, and plants respond to this by growing rapidly. Clear, sunny skies and light breezes punctuated by devastating thunderstorms are typical. Storm water can pan your soil: mulch with peat or compost to keep workable.

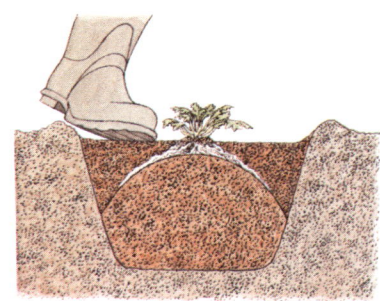
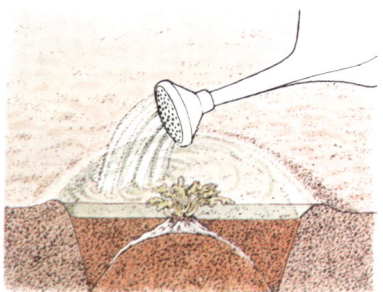
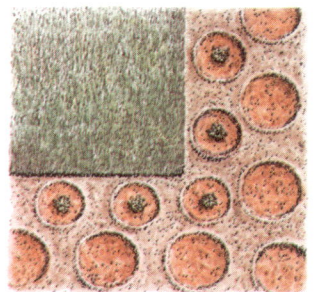

Project work: starting the herbaceous border: starting a beautiful lawn

Perennials are the most reliable source of colour in your garden. They will go on year after year giving you a wonderful show, getting bigger and better with the passing of time. It takes all sorts to make a garden, just as it takes all sorts to make a world. Buy your plants dormant from your garden centre. Leave them overnight in a bucket of water, still wrapped in their paper. Dawn next day, dig over the bed as recommended in Stage 2, picking out stones, roots; add moss peat and bone meal. Then dig an individual hole for each plant, a spade's blade deep and a spade's blade across. Scatter the soil on the bed. Then make a hill at the bottom of the hole. You want to plant the dahlia tuber with its top 4 in. below soil level, so make the hill with soilless growing mix, rounding it up till the tuber is at the right level. Level off hole with more soilless growing mix. Firm, leaving a saucer-shaped depression. Soak. Plant the chrysanthemums the same way, except that you will need to make the soilless growing mix hills higher, so that the sprouting tops of the chrysanthemums are above soil level. Spread the roots over the hill, in-fill with more soilless growing mix, firm, soak. Soak both lots of plants twice, then rake surplus soil from rim back over depression. Next lawns. A good lawn is essential to any garden: it shows off the flowers like well-polished shoes show off a good suit. Over the next weeks we'll be giving you some ideas for changing your lawn from a patch of coarse grass or bare earth and weeds into a springy lawn to be proud of. Begin by feeding and mowing your lawn regularly. It'll start looking better in next to no time. Dig out small weeds like daisies with a daisy fork: larger weeds with a trowel. Fill hole with soilless growing mix and firm really hard.

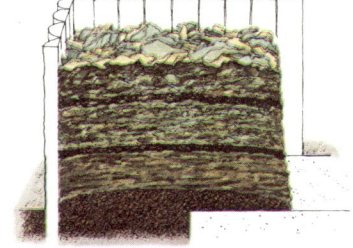

Stage 6

This fortnight we make a start on the first of the permanent features in our garden – the patio. It's a great asset, for sitting out, eating out, enjoying relaxation in the sun. Not hard work if you take it gently. Bull-at-a-gate techniques will give you backache for months. Slow and easy does it. Extend the time budget if you need to. Also some bright ideas on what to do with the soil you dig out. Some other novelties too.

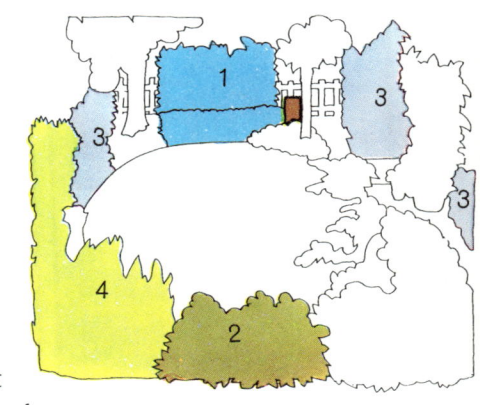

Needs list: *broken brick/gravel/coarse sand; square wooden pegs; 1 ball string; 1 spirit level; 1 pkt nasturtium seed; 1 pkt Canary creeper seed.*
Time budget: *6 hours in 2 weeks*

Flower of the Fortnight

Here's another high-speed annual to provide instant screening, the ornamental hop – *Humulus japonicus* 'Variegatus'. It's variegated, which means the leaves are splashed white and cream as well as green: beautiful! It's a twiner, so it needs supports to climb. Twines clockwise. Take a pencil, wind a piece of string round it clockwise. Note the string ascends from right to left. Botanists say it ascends left to right. That's because they're looking outwards from inside the pencil. Crazy? No. They're just trying to solve a problem. South of the Equator this plant twines anticlockwise: like the bath water running out business you know. For planting procedures, see Stage 3.

Groundwork

1 Time to meet two of the creepiest, crawliest, slimiest and most destructive of all garden pests – slugs and snails. There's nothing sluggish about slugs when it comes to eating their way through the stems of your favourite garden plants, and snails don't move at a snail's pace when it comes to eating plants either. Both set to work at night, which makes them harder to catch, and they often do their damage just underground, so you don't see the damage, only that the plant is dead. By day they hide in dark, cool, moist parts of the garden. Catch them by placing a tile or slat $1\frac{1}{2}$ in. above soaked earth, put lettuce leaves or half orange under, largely cover with earth: two weeks later remove, scrape slugs and snails off underside with a board into incinerator. 2 The sword-like leaves of the gladioli should be up by now. Sow left-over annual seeds between them to cover bed. Reseed bare patches in the annual bed. 3 Check the height of the lawn-mower cut: aim for a blade height of $\frac{3}{4}$ in. Keep all seeds moist, in semi-shade and labelled.

Mid June weather/soil

The longest day of the year approaches, but summer still lags behind. There are hot days yet to come in July and August. More northerly districts benefit most now from the long days, and at last catch up with more southerly areas. Still not too late to sow seeds that failed first go.

Project work: starting the patio: some original ideas

The British and Americans face a peculiar gardening dilemma other nationals don't seem to have: is a garden a place in which to garden or to relax? The French, Spanish, Italians are quite decided: it is a secluded place in which to relax. From the Taj Mahal through the Persian gardens to the Moorish gardens of Spain, gardens are for relaxation. A good garden combines work with a rest place. A patio. Time to start making it, start using up that growing pile or bin of stones you've been weeding out of the borders. First peg out your patio area with stakes and string. Ours is 6 ft. by 4 ft. – including the garden path. Excavate the patio area 6 in. deep. Put excavated soil to one side for use on the rockery/rock garden later. (Borrow a wheelbarrow if you don't have one.) Cover the bottom 4 in. deep in large stones, hard core. Then cover with 1 in. smaller stones. Then a 1 in. layer of builder's sand. Schedule your work so the path can be used while work is in progress. Make level. Since you've got all this soil out of your patio area, use it for something useful. Make a mound of it, and plant potatoes in it. Use sprouting seed spuds, and plant 4 in. deep. Sow seeds of climbing nasturtiums (*Nasturtium major*) which come in a riot of colours. Buy a packet of mixed colours and sow seed like the sunflower seeds (Stage 4) but press 1 in. down. Also sow seeds of Canary climber to use in tubs, containers, later. Blanch the leaves of any dandelions growing in the garden by placing a large flower pot over them. Any dandelions will do – but proper culinary ones are best. Never eat leaves of dandelions off the lawn. You never know what weedkillers someone else may have used on them. Lastly, save your toilet roll tubes, halve, fill with soil-less growing mix, put in box of soil, sow annuals in them. Restricting roots produces small, colourful flowers.

 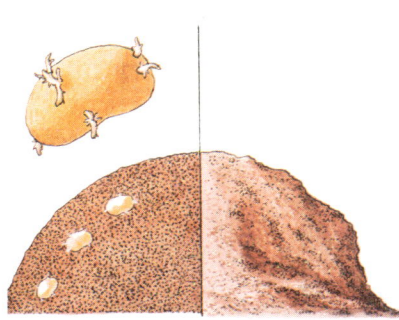

Stage 7

We devote the bulk of Stage 7 to finishing your patio. It seems a shame having started not to keep on going and get it finished. If you're a warm weather gardener, you need to do it now because cold weather will deter you later. In parts of the US you freeze solid in winter you've little option. In the UK and in mild winter zones of the US you could leave this till mid winter, when the plants are making the least demands on you.

Needs list: *15 pre-cast concrete paving slabs; 1 bag cement/sand mix; 4 lengths used board 4 in by 1½ in; four 15 in stakes; 2 transplants each of the herbs you want.*
Time budget: *7 hours in 2 weeks*

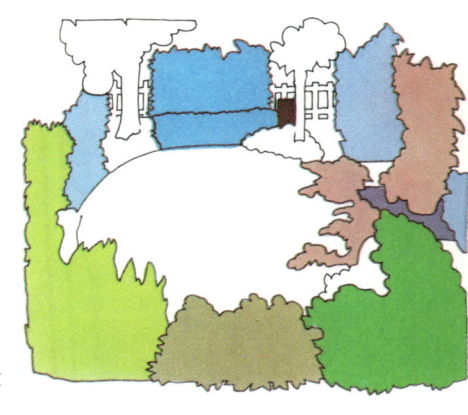

Flower of the Fortnight

This fortnight's gaily coloured flower is probably known to you as a geranium. It's not a geranium. A geranium is something else again. It's a pelargonium. Ask for a geranium and you might just get the wrong plant. Pelargoniums are a huge group of sun-loving South Africans. The flowers come in colours from white through pinks to scarlet, crimson, mauve and dusky blacks. The leaves are almost as varied, sometimes just with a brown stripe, often with concentric rings of red, yellow, green, white and brown. Some creep, crawl, climb or sprawl. All are delightful, all ways, always. Ideal for tubs, pots, hanging baskets, troughs, sinks and so on. Ask your garden centre for advice on varieties.

Groundwork

1 Remove dead heads of annuals to extend flowering season. 2 Continue to mow lawn regularly: most people mow once a week; keen gardeners twice a week; fanatics three times a week. Continue to dig out large weeds as in Stage 5. 3 Check compost bin for continuing decomposition of vegetable matter. Sprinkle a layer of commercial activator on top if you don't seem to be getting results. 4 Moisture conservation: very important. Hoe top 1 in. of soil to make a 'blanket' of fine soil particles. Leave hoed weeds on ground as a green mulch. 5 Keep newly planted bedding plants moist. Alternative bedding plants include petunias, ageratum, tagetes, salvia, coleus, trailing nepeta, pansy and French marigold. 6 Friends and foes. Ants are enemies. They 'farm' aphids for their 'honey'. Sprinkle sugar, watch ants carry it to their nest, then destroy nest with boiling water. Centipedes are friends: they eat many troublesome bugs. Don't jump on them just because they look as though they might be a pest. There are enough real pests to jump on as it is.

Early July weather/soil

High air and soil temperatures keep plants growing well. High air temperatures cause the plants to draw heavily on soil-water reserves so keep the hose sprinkling in hot, dry weather. Summer vacation can wreck your gardening schedule, so plan with a neighbour to see to essentials.

Project work: the patio and the herb garden

If you want to press on with your patio, here's how to go about it. It's fun to get it finished at this time of year – you can use it right away. Choose paving materials to suit your home. We've chosen 2 ft. by 2 ft. non-slip pre-cast concrete paving slabs. We lay ours four square. The patio area (Stage 6) should now be extended to 8 ft. by 6 ft. to take 12 slabs. Do your own sums for your own materials. Use stakes, string, boards and spirit level to check patio level. Allow slight slope so water drains away from house: allow a fall of ½ in. in 6 ft. Fill and firm any hollows in hard core. Rake layer of builder's sand level (allowing for fall). Allow for thickness of paving slabs when lining levels up with existing paths &c.' about 2½ in. Mix cement/sand and lay 5 dollops for each slab – one under each corner, one under middle. Position slab on cement. Tamp down. Check levels two ways with spirit level. Lay slabs row by row. Leave ½ in. between slabs. Fill later with strong cement/sand mix. Rake out footmarks and re-level sand before laying next row. Complete laying slabs. A week later fill gaps between slabs. Add finishing touch. Lay 3 slabs in the lawn. Set them in the lawn as described in Stage 10. Then the mower will go over them easily. Next make your herb garden. Make a board frame as illustrated. Fix size to suit your garden. Creosote wood. Fix extra boards across middle to make a compartmented herb garden if you want: helps control runaway herbs like mint. Place in position. Save money: use patio levelling stakes as corner stakes for herb garden. Once frame is in position, place a 3 in. drainage layer across the bottom. Fill frame with soilless growing mix. Firm. Leave to settle. Do not plant your herbs till the spring. Buy pot-grown plants or grow from seed sown in peat pots indoors during the winter months. Alternatively root cuttings of shrubby herbs in late summer to overwinter indoors.

Stage 8

This fortnight we start on the second of our two major, permanent shape-changing tasks. The first was making the patio. Now it's time to make the lawn look so good it'll be the envy of others in your street. You'll see. We plan to change the shape of the lawn to a circle. Once you've done yours, don't be surprised if other people try to copy yours. This one change will do more to improve your garden than any other single change.

Needs list: *1 pkt broad bean seed; 1 pkt snap bean seed; 1 bundle stakes.*
Time budget: *6 hours in 2 weeks*

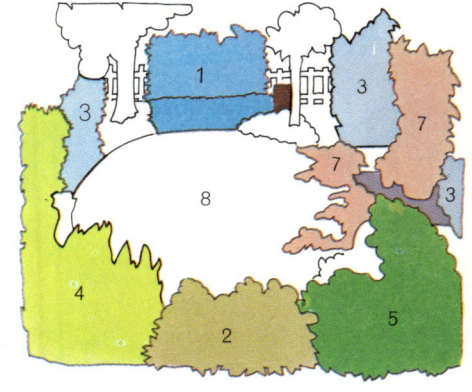

Flower of the Fortnight

The ideal small tree for a small garden should have brilliantly fresh green or shrimp pink young leaves in spring, flamboyant flowers in early summer, eye-catching fruits in late summer, fiery leaf colour in fall and stunning bark to hold your interest through winter. Trouble is, there's no one tree that does all of these things. If you've got a small garden – only room for one tree – choose one that has more of these attributes than any other you can find. Probably the nearest comer is a yellow-fruiting crab apple, *Malus* 'Golden Hornet': spring leaves pinkish: flowers early summer, pale pink, prolific; fruits late summer, eye-catching golden-yellow: reddish-purple leaves in fall.

Groundwork

1 Check compost bin. The layers you first put in should be starting to look like good moss peat, light and crumbly to the touch. 2 Continue removing large weeds from the lawn, and keep on cutting it regularly. Now's the time to repeat the feeding if the lawn feed you used requires a second dosage. Concentrate your watering on newly planted plants and newly turfed lawn. 4 Remove the strongest seedlings from the seed box (Stage 6), lifting with a kitchen fork to make sure you take earth with the roots. Put transplants one to a peat pot, filling the peat pots with a soilless potting mix. Water in. 5 Check on patio levels. Top up any subsidence. 6 If any young sunflowers or vines have failed, sow replacements, and waste no time about it. 7 If your annuals are not in flower yet, clear the bed and sow replacements to flower in late fall. 8 If your bag of moss peat has dried out, soak it so the peat's wet when you want to use it. 9 Heavy rains may flatten some plants. Stake them upright again; refirm soil round stems. Use hoe to break soil crust.

Mid July weather/soil

Usually the hottest time of the year, this can be marvellous in the garden if there's sufficient rain to keep growth lush. In dry years bottom leaves will tend to turn brown. Rain, when it comes, can be very heavy, so make sure tall plants are staked securely otherwise they'll break.

 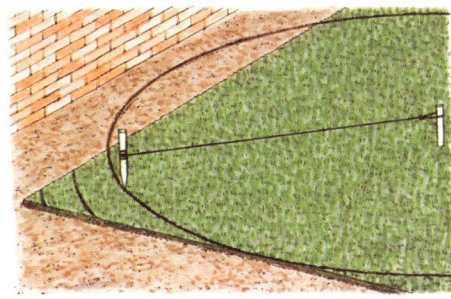 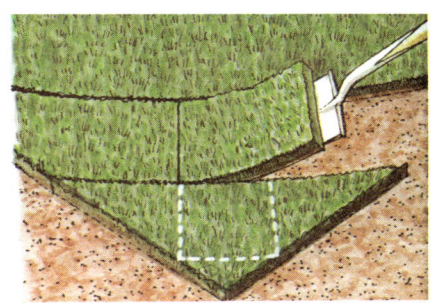

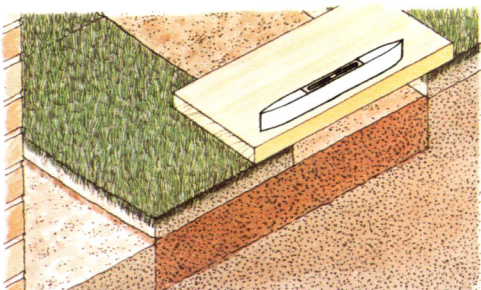 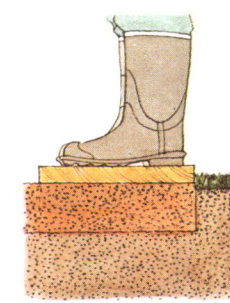

Project work: our new lawn shape; more vegetables

A lawn needs to be more than merely green and level and well-mown to look great. It needs to be the right shape for the garden it belongs in. House and garden are one entity: home. Just about everything in the home is square or squared – the doors, the windows, the rooms, the house itself, everything from foundations to fence are basically square. So, unfortunately, are most lawns. Break away from that shape, round your lawn, and everything else will relax and flow with it. Our lawn is round. If you have a very long garden, have two round lawns. Decide the diameter of the lawn to fit your garden. Ours is 15 ft. Find the centre point of your new lawn. Stick a stake dead centre. Tie a string to it. Tie a peg to the end of the string at the precise radius needed ($\frac{1}{2}$ your diameter). Scratch a circle in the turf. Dig and prepare areas to be re-turfed as in Stage 1. With your spade held upright, cut cleanly, following the line of your circle. Then cut parallel lines in the outer part of your lawn, 12 in. apart. Remove turf outside circle – in lengths of not more than 18 in. Lift by pushing your spade under the turf. Use these turves to shape new parts of the lawn. Stack any surplus turves to rot down for the rockery. Check levels with spirit level laid on a board. Switch to your vegetable patch. Make a tripod of poles for your pole beans, and tie them in. Dig new holes for a second crop of dwarf French or bush snap beans. Plant firmly. Water in.

Stage 9

This is one of those rare fortnights when you have a lot you could learn, but relatively little that you actually need to do; so make the most of it. We show you how to plant gladiolus – a typical corm, plus telling you something of its curious natural history. We remind you how to stake your dahlias. Then back to the lawn. Lawns need constant attention, no matter how well you make them in the first place. We look at filling hollows and flattening bumps in your lawn.

Needs list: *1 bag organic garden manure; 25 gladioli corms; ½ cwt/50 lb bag soilless growing mix; 12 French marigold plants; twelve 3 ft canes; 1 pkt plant ties.*
Time budget: *2 hours in 2 weeks*

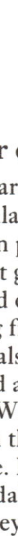

Flower of the Fortnight

Dahlias are one of the most spectacular and diverse of all groups of garden plants. There are different sorts that grow from 9 in. to 10 ft. high, and come with flowers anything from 1 in. to 12 in. across, with petals spiked, rounded, fluted scalloped and many more – single or double. What's more there's every colour in the rose rainbow – except true blue. No wonder people became dahlia buffs! The surprise is that they're not modern plants but natives of Mexico. The basic breeding was done by the Aztecs, who held them sacred. Coming from Mexico, they're frost tender: plant in spring, lift in fall: store in dry peat or sand boxes over winter. Start with the bushy, 3 ft. pom-pom types.

Groundwork

By now you should have a good idea of whether or not your battle against the weeds is being successful. Check on the methods shown in Stage 4. If you really resent weeds because they look untidy rather than because they may be unduly harming your plants, you may find hard weeding is the only satisfactory solution. But you'll know by the end of the summer just how much – or how little – of your garden you can take care of in this way. There are chemical methods of controlling weeds, and both these and the chemicals you may want to use for killing bugs are discussed elsewhere. In general, the less chemicals you use in your garden the better. Without being fanatical about it, it is just worth remembering that most of the chemicals now sold for killing weeds or bugs were originally developed as nerve gases – to kill humans: so treat them with the respect they deserve. Learn some more friends and foes: spiders are friends, eat your enemies for you: worms aerate soil, help soil breathe. All caterpillars are enemies: they eat your plants.

Early August weather/soil

Many plants are already past their best, though there are plenty still to come. Many of those already over will come again if you cut them back, liquid feed and water lavishly. Still 3 months to go before frosts, and the soil is warm enough for rapid seed germination – worth a try.

  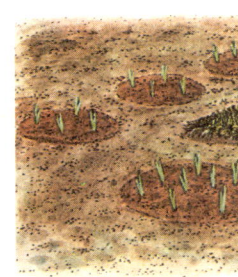

Project work: planting gladioli; the natural history of corms; staking dahlias; keeping the lawn looking perfect

Gladioli, often known as sword lilies – though they are not lilies at all – are among the most spectacular of high to late summer-flowering plants. The sorts usually grown are hybrids of complex parentage, crossed from mainly South African species. These are the big growing gladioli. The smaller ones, the primulinas, butterfly gladioli and so on are derived mainly from cornfield weeds from Spain southwards. All are typical corms. A corm, like a bulb, is an underground storage organ. Foodstuffs accumulated during one growing season are stored in the corm over winter, and supply the foodstuffs needed to start it into growth next year. Most gladioli are frost tender, so you need to lift them and store them in a dry, frost-free place over winter. Some are hardy. And if you leave them in the ground you'll find they 'walk'. They'll come up in a different place each year. Plant gladioli as

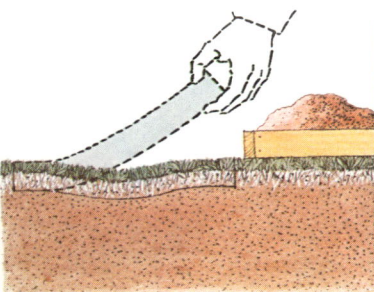 

shown in the illustrations, 3 to a hole, bedded on soilless growing mix and covered above with soilless growing mix. Use the same technique for all corms. For a good show dig 4 holes each 12 in. diameter and 6 in. deep. Two ways you can stake your dahlias. Either tie in one plant per stake, or make a tripod, train 3 plants up it. Probably gives you the best massed show. Look after your lawn. First check levels. An eye-check will do, but use a spirit level if you're a perfectionist. To fill

hollows lever up lawn gently with a spade, fill hollow with soilless growing mix, replace lawn, firm. Remove high points similarly by lifting grass, chopping height off soil, then returning grass. Hard lawns need aerating. Spike with garden fork, pressing it 3–4 in. into the lawn, in straight rows. Work across the lawn first one way then the opposite way. Or buy yourself a roller type aerator.

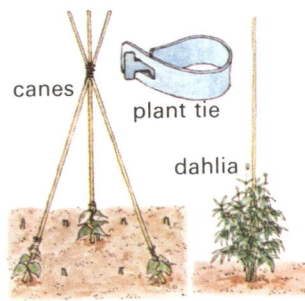 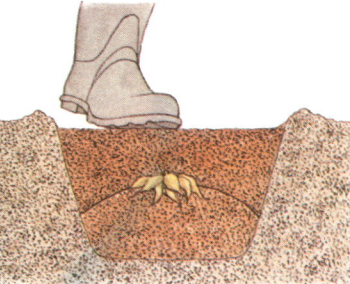

Stage 10

A really original feature heads the project work this week, as we edge our new circular lawn with one of the many decorative concrete paving slabs available. We select a slate-grey type from the many colours on the market. We start by edging the area where the cottage garden is going to be. Although getting late in the season, there's just time to plant a last crop of quick-growing vegetables and to sow wallflower seed to flower next spring.

Needs list: *1 bag sharp sand; 10 pre-cast concrete paving slabs; 1 pkt wallflower seed; 1 pkt lettuce seed (or carrot or radish).*
Time budget: *4 hours in 1 week*

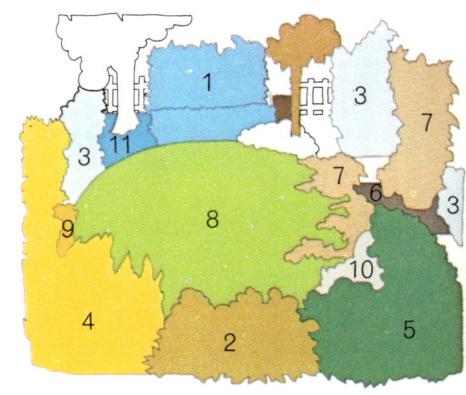

Flower of the Fortnight
The wallflower is without doubt one of the world's top ten old-fashioned favourite flowers. It's been known and grown in European gardens since the Dark Ages, and is widely naturalised in many places. A quick look at wallflowers growing wild gives you a good idea of the sort of conditions they need in your garden: you'll nearly always find them growing on cliffs or in the mortar of old walls. So their first need is perfect drainage. They also enjoy chalk or lime – but it's not necessary to add any if you have an acid soil. They're biennials, growing to sturdy little plants in their first year, then flowering, seeding and dying their second. Grown for their scent as much as their lovely velvety flowers.

Groundwork
1 Time to harvest dwarf French or bush snap beans. When the beans are shelled, save the young pods. Dice into a little salted boiling water, cover, cook $\frac{1}{4}$ hour, strain; keep the liquid for your own white sauce recipe. 2 Make notes of any plants you see in the neighbourhood which take your fancy. Classify them into the kinds illustrated opposite. Find out the name whenever possible. 3 Water plants badly affected by drought. Pay particular attention to newly planted plants and to plants growing in containers. Plants growing in containers need feeding too. Use a proprietary liquid feed: get advice on what's best from your garden centre. Keep a very special watch on seedlings. They are the most vulnerable to drought. Water before they wilt, but never keep too wet. Continue learning about your garden friends and foes. If you find a toad in your garden, don't scream. It's a friend, one of the greatest of all enemy insect eaters. Make sure you don't disturb its lair: keep it cool, protected and sheltered. Don't handle the toad unnecessarily.

Mid August weather/soil
The gardener's year is on the turn by now, though there's still more summer to come. Most plants respond to the urge to form seed, fruit; some are already shedding their seeds. Shorter day length is noticeable, and dawn and dusk are definitely colder than a couple of weeks ago.

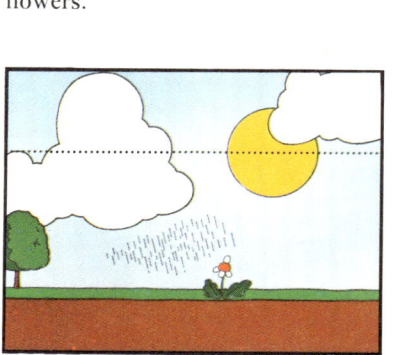

Project work: edging the lawn; sowing seed

Now for the really smart bit about your lawn. Edging it with concrete paving slabs. First, check the exact diameter of your lawn. Go back to Stage 8 and go through the same measuring process again. Position slabs where you want them, 18 in. apart. Admire the effect. Mark position of each slab, then stack out of the way. Dig holes bigger than the slabs, at least 6 in. deep. Fill with brick/stones/rubble. Make firm. Cover with ½ in. layer builder's sand. Bed slabs on that. Set them just below the grass level so that your mower will clear them. Back fill and ram soil firm. Adjust slab levels with extra sand. Sow wallflower seed in drills: transplant later.

Recognizing plant types. A plant is a plant is a plant but. It does help your gardening if you can recognize the basic types. Let's start with an annual. Little things, fast growing, from seed, to flower to seed and dead in a season. (4) Cheap, but often self-seed in your garden. A biennial takes 2 seasons to do the same thing. A perennial (2) has permanent roots and makes top-growth annually, dying back each winter. A bulb (3) is a special type of perennial which stores its food over winter in a swollen underground bud – the bulb. Usually inexpensive. Often in flower when few other plants are – e.g., early spring, late fall. Shrubs (1) technically woody perennials. Get bigger year by year. A good investment. Choose carefully: they last a lifetime.

Stage 11

The first plants to go into the cottage garden/perennial area will add to our collection of permanent plants, which started with the gladiolus (corm), the dahlia (tuber) and the Korean chrysanthemum. First choices are periwinkle and thyme, because they are low-growing and spread to carpet the ground, making new plants as they go. We prepare our tree pit but back fill it so nobody falls in by mistake. Easy enough to re-excavate when the tree does arrive.

Needs list: *One $\frac{1}{2}$ cwt/50 lb bag moss peat; 4 periwinkle plants; 6 thyme plants.*
Time budget: *4 hours in 1 week*

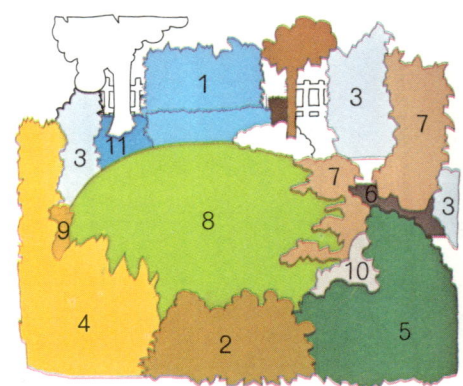

Flower of the Fortnight

Most of the plants in the early gardens both of Europe and America were herbs or wild flowers, collected from meadows, woods and hedgerows and then cultivated. The periwinkle, *Vinca minor*, is one such wild flower of Europe brought into cultivation centuries ago. A marvellous plant, with glossy evergreen leaves and green stems that arch and root where they touch the ground, making, in time, large mats that keep the weeds down. Grows anywhere, any soil, sun or shade, and is nearly always in flower. There are forms with leaves variegated silver or gold. Though the flower is usually sky blue, there are forms with white flowers, purple flowers and even double flowers. Chop plants back if they get too big.

Groundwork

1 Keep all containers well watered, also marrows/squashes, tomatoes and other high water content vegetables. Elsewhere use water with restraint: only water when necessary. 2 Trim faded parts of annuals, vines and bedding plants. 3 Work compost from your own heap into the surface of the soil in the gladiolus bed. If the ground is really dry, soak it first. 4 If you have neglected your weeding, go out into your garden and look at your weeds. You'll find they're covered in seed pods – all ready to start another crop of weeds for later in the year. Old saying: one year's seeds make 7 years weeds. Be warned. Weed immediately. 5 Your lawn may be starting to look brown and scorched. It will recover quickly after rain. Only water newly turfed areas. Dry spells keep the moss in check. 6 Learn about a few more friends and foes. Earwigs are especially destructive to dahlias. Loosely fill a peat pot with paper, place on top of stake. Remove paper every few days and burn it, with the insects in it. Renew paper. Bees are friends: just don't disturb their nest.

Late August weather/soil

First hints of autumn tint this week's weather, with heavy dews and often misty nights. All truly summer plants are over, and autumn flowering ones have not yet reached their best, which is why so many gardens look rather jaded round now. Harvest seeds and fruits, tidy tired plants.

Project work: of lots of things, but mainly looking forward to our tree

If you've already got a large tree in your garden, casting dense shade, look on it with affection: it may stop you growing some plants but it'll help you grow others. Don't plant close to the trunk, but keep an area under the fringe of the branches for your cottage garden perennial plants. Dig holes 6 in. deep, trim any roots you find with pruning shears/secateurs, and fill holes with soilless growing mix. Plant periwinkle, and others as recommended in Stage 5. Plant thyme between the paving slabs round your lawn. 6 in. hole, soilless growing mix. You know the drill. Space plants 8 in. apart. They'll grow together. Plant more periwinkle outside the slabs. 6 in. hole, soilless growing mix &c. Space 12 in. apart. Firm. Soak. Next, make up your own high nitrogen fertilizer. Crush eggshells from the kitchen, leave them in a plastic bucket of water for 2 weeks or longer. Use the resulting liquid as a liquid feed. Don't use on acid-loving plants. Next consider your tree and where it will grow. The site was determined earlier on the plan. Check it again. Trees take a lot of planting. If they're in the wrong place, they take a lot of moving. Stick a rake in the ground, handle end down, to give you some idea what your tree position really means – where the shade falls, what it hides. Mark out hole 3 ft. across: use stake/string/peg method for marking hole (see Stage 8). Lift turf: see Stage 8. Stack turf for rockery later. Dig hole 18 in. deep. Dig sides straight down. Flat bottom. Break up soil at bottom. Fill back mixing peat with the soil. Surplus soil to rockery/rock garden area. Don't firm hole. Just let soil settle itself. Later, when you plant the tree, make sure the soil is just below the soil level the tree was growing at before. If you get earth above that the bark will rot and the tree will die. You'll find that the root/trunk junction is just above ground.

47

Stage 12

We continue stocking up the cottage garden area with meadow saffron – *Colchicum autumnale* – sometimes wrongly known as autumn crocus. The crocus-like flowers come in August/September, the huge leaves in spring. Plant the corm as soon as you buy it, or put it on a window sill to flower – no earth, no water – then plant out to let it make leaf. Having done turfing earlier, we now prepare a piece of ground for seeding for a lawn in autumn.

Needs list: *3 colchicum corms; 1 pkt compost activator.*
Time budget: *1 hour in 1 week*

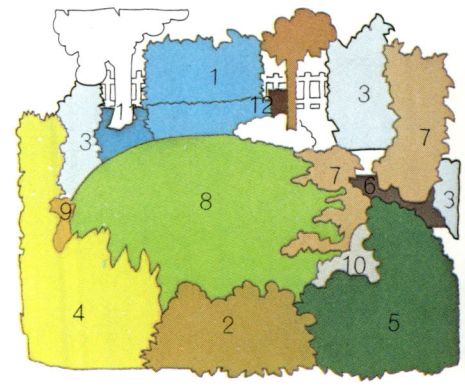

Early September weather/soil

Autumn is arriving rapidly now, announcing itself in a whirl of equinoxial gales, tearing fiery leaves from trees. Starry nights are followed by heavy dews caused by the air being colder than the soil. Good time to plant since roots can get established before the soil cools.

Flower of the Fortnight

Colchicums are the most spectacular plant in flower in the garden in their season. They're so easy to grow well that the surprising thing is that you don't see them in every garden. Often known as autumn crocuses, they're not crocuses at all. Autumn crocuses are true crocuses: colchicums merely look like crocuses: actually they're first cousins to the lilies, though you'd never guess it to look at them. The great fat corms produce a succession of crocus-like flowers from bare ground in fall. The large strap-shaped leaves follow in spring. The easiest to grow is *Colchicum autumnale*, but there are other species and varieties with purple or white flowers, and some with double flowers.

Groundwork

1 Often a hot, dry time of year now, so keep on watering all containers, and essential plants like marrows, tomatoes, pumpkins. Save water when you can. Use washing-up water on marrows/squashes and tomatoes: does the plants no harm, helps to kill soil bugs. 2 Pinch out growing tips of marrows/squashes and tomatoes to keep plants compact and help fruits to form. 3 Check for wallflower seedlings around the garden, identify them, mark them with stakes to move later if you want to. 4 Work a good layer of peat into the surface of the soil in the dahlia and chrysanthemum bed: if it's very dry, soak first. 5 Learn about a few more friends and enemies. Dogs and cats may be your best friends, but they're not your garden's best friends. Learn to control them. The British hedgehog is definitely a garden's good friend. As is America's praying mantis. They have a voracious appetite for insects. Don't try to tame a hedgehog. If you do it's very likely it may emerge prematurely from hibernation, and that could kill it. In America you can buy the large egg-cases of praying mantis to hatch in the garden.

Project work: the cottage garden/perennial patch
Plant your colchicum corms under the shade of a large, existing tree.

Use trowel to dig straight-sided holes at least 8 in. deep. Put 4 in soilless growing mix in bottom for the roots to grow into. Press

corms firmly down. Cover with more soilless growing mix. Firm. Soak. Large leaves cover the ground in spring.

 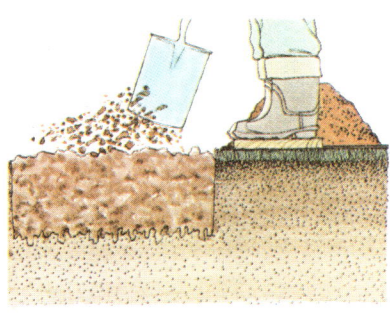 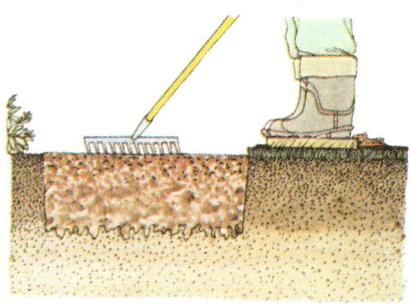

Prepare ground for grass seeding by digging over the soil, removing

stones, roots &c. Break up sub-soil but don't bring it to the surface.

Sprinkle moss peat/sand/soil mix Use a board to protect turf.

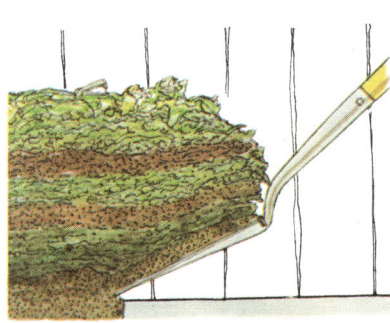

If your soil's heavy clay or pure rubble, remove top 4 in. and replace with better soil from the rockery/ rock garden heap.

Stage 13

Tree planting time has arrived so it's time to re-excavate the tree pit we dug earlier and plant our tree. Don't worry if yours does not arrive the day you expected it: nurserymen have literally thousands of orders to send off. Be patient: your tree will come. Plant any time in fall when the ground is not too wet or not frozen solid. Staking and tying are very important: we show you how to do it right. With your tree planted, you're half way home in your garden.

Needs list: *1 tree stake; 1 strong tree tie, 1 pkt honesty seed.*
Time budget: *4 hours in 2 weeks*

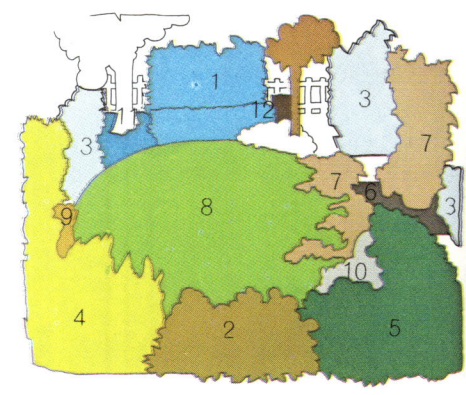

Late September weather/soil

Calm, warm days, often very sunny, typify this season's weather: plants can suffer drought. Still nights encourage dew and even frost to form. Stray gales remind one autumn is still with us. Take back indoors house plants stood out for the summer. Keep lawn well mown right into winter.

Flower of the Fortnight

Honesty (*Lunaria biennis*) is about the nearest thing there is to a desirable weed. It will seed itself readily in your garden, but is no problem. You'll soon learn to recognize the young plants with their attractive bright green, heart-shaped leaves. Just pull out the seedlings growing where you don't want them. Leave them where you do. Like the wallflower (Stage 10) honesty is a biennial: little plant first year, flowers and seed second year: finished. It's grown as much for its coin-shaped, silvery, papery seed cases which last indefinitely indoors as dried flower decorations as for its showy heads of pink flowers. If you let seedlings grow on, you'll get some with pure white flowers.

Groundwork

1 Collect seed from Shirley poppies, calendulas, nasturtiums, Canary creeper and sunflowers to sow next year. Dead head calendulas, pelargoniums, fuchsias, petunias &c – there's often a mini-spring in the fall – lots of fresh flowers. 3 Pinch back convolvulus and hope to encourage growth low down. 4 Check stakes are secure on gladioli and chrysanthemums. 5 Keep thyme and periwinkle well watered till established. 6 Tie in straggly shoots on pole beans – they'll soon be in fruit. 7 Pinch out new growths on tomatoes, marrows/squashes, so that the plants concentrate on fruit production. Keep these vegetables well watered. Move tomato bags to the warmest, sunniest place in your garden. 8 Thin out carrots, radishes, lettuces: use thinnings to flavour salads, stews, broths. 9 Top up hollows in newly laid turf, using a soil/sand mix. 10 Watch out for late crop of weed seedlings and hoe them out of existence as soon as they appear. 11 Mulch your newly planted tree with lawn clippings, moss peat or compost from your own compost heap: keep watered.

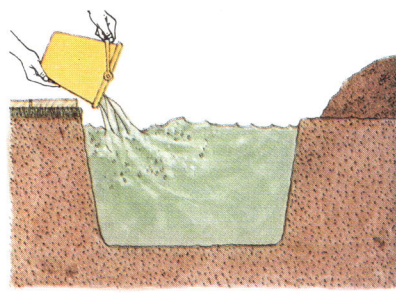
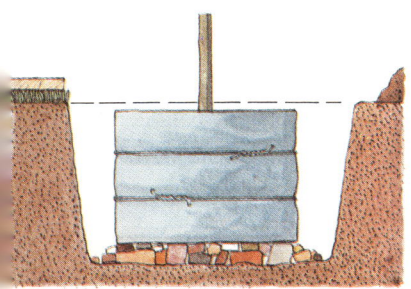
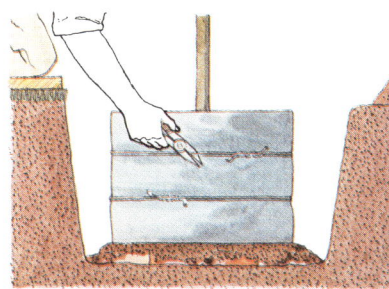
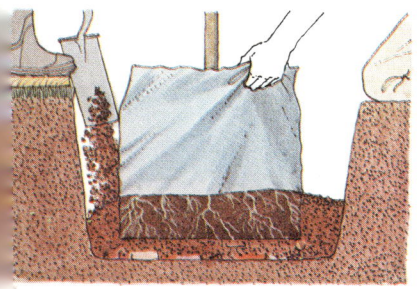
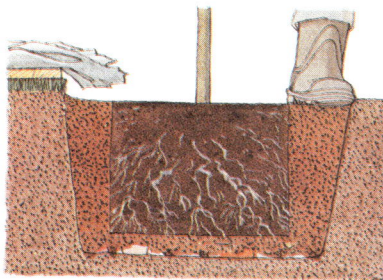

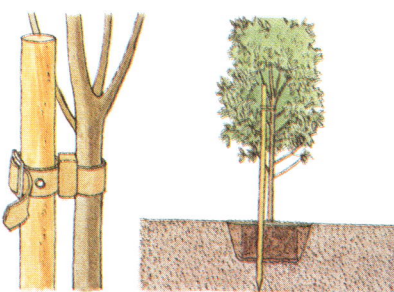

Project work: planting the tree

Any day now the container-grown tree you ordered should arrive. If you forgot to order, it's still not too late to get your garden centre to deliver one for you. Trees come in several types of container – but you treat them all much the same. When the tree arrives, put it in a shaded, sheltered place with sacking/burlap over its roots. Use the garage, garden shed, whatever. Prevents frost or wind damage. Re-excavate the tree pit dug earlier (Stage 11). If you intend to heap the earth out on to the lawn, protect the grass by putting boards down first. Once the pit is excavated, fill it with water, then leave for 3 days before planting. Next lay bricks/stones/rubble as a drainage layer for the tree. Move the tree in its container to the edge of the pit. Lift it by the container, not by the stem. Takes two people to move it. Lower tree in container into hole. Adjust level by sliding bricks, stones &c. under container. Cut wires round container. Slide out base sheet of container if there is one. Start back filling with soil you excavated earlier. Wriggle container gently upwards as you fill. Firm soil every 6 in. Fill till the soil is level with the soil in the container. Firm soil again, leaving slight depression. Don't soak. Get wife/friend to hold stem aside and drive sharpened stake vertically into the ground. The stake should go well below the drainage layer. It should go in vertically, parallel with the tree stem, about $1\frac{1}{2}$ in. from it. Tie firmly just below main branches. Make sure no branches can rub against the stake. Take a coffee break. Then come back and soak the depression thoroughly. Finally sit back and admire your work. The success of your tree will depend on how well you planted it. A well-excavated hole, with plenty of fresh soil for the roots to grow into, will thrive. Year 1 it won't do a lot. Year 2 it will grow rapidly. Year 3 it will settle down to flowering and fruiting.

51

6 Months in

After 6 months and a mere 52 hours work, does your garden look like our artist's impression of how our baseplan garden should look now? Does it look any different from when you started? Did you take any colour shots of your garden before you started work, like we suggested? And if you did, can you find them, take some more, from the same positions, and then compare the results? That's the only real way to check your progress. If you've kept up with your project work and your groundwork, you should be feeling rather excited by what you've achieved.

If your garden doesn't look quite as colourful as this picture, don't worry. Artists' impressions have a way of making things look more exciting and more colourful than they really are. Your own photos are your best guide to how you have succeeded.

With luck you've managed to keep abreast of all the project work and the groundwork too. However, if you haven't don't worry. The whole plan is flexible. Any areas you have neglected, any projects you haven't had time to keep up with, abandon for this year. Start them from scratch next year. For the rest of this year, just keep on with the project work in the areas of the garden where you have been able to cope. Also abandon any parts of the garden that you think may be too much to deal with over the coming 6 months, and leave them too till next year.

So far we've been on a crash programme to revitalize your soil and bring instant colour and cover to the garden. Over the next 6 months we'll turn these instant but temporary effects into permanent plantings and concentrate on making a garden that will look good for years to come with little further trouble.

Meanwhile, we're reporting on how our 6 volunteer gardeners, did over their first 6 months. From our point of view, the Thorpes' and the Allans' gardens were most successful, because they had to start from scratch, with average conditions, and were able to follow every stage. Others had to be selective because their gardens were too established, too shaded, too small or for some similar reason. But all of them – as well as their neighbours – agree they have been stimulated into seeing their gardens in a new and fascinating light. You'll find out how they fared on the following pages.

Recap of workplans 1-13

Colour key code recap
1 = Bean bed
2 = Annuals bed
3 = Covering vines
4 = Summer display bed
5 = Autumn display bed
6 = Patio
7 = Container plants
8 = Lawn
9 = Summer bedding plants
10 = Vegetable patch
11 = Cottage garden/perennial corner
12 = Compost bin
13 = Ornamental tree
14 = Bulb bed
15 = Trellis
16 = Permanent ground cover
17 = Living hedge
18 = Shrub bed
19 = Herbaceous border
20 = Climbing roses
21 = Herb bed
22 = Fan-trained tree
23 = Decoration
24 = Rockery/rock garden
25 = Patio paving
26 = Christmas present plants

This page is simply a resume of pages 12/13 – an instant guide to the colours and numbers that relate to workplans 1–13 – your first 6 months. Use it to check your own progress, and to remind yourself of the meaning of each number and colour as you check on the progress of the 6 volunteer gardeners. Use it too, to see how the basic groundplan was adapted to fit the different needs of the different gardens and their owners.

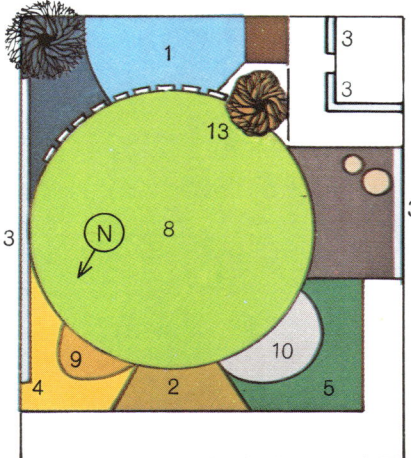

The numbers and key colours on the plan (above) and tracing (left) refer to the components of the garden (right). Each chart will be discussed in detail during the growing season; the sequence will not be exactly the same as this diagrammatic order here.

The Trial Gardens

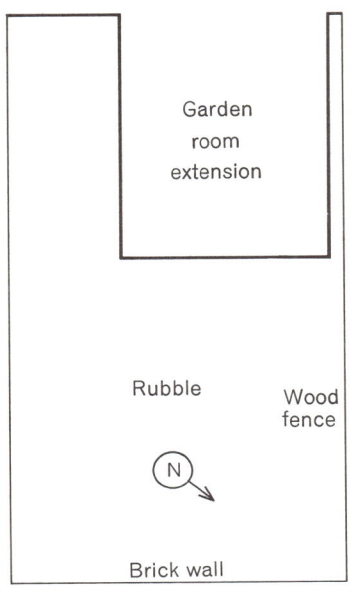
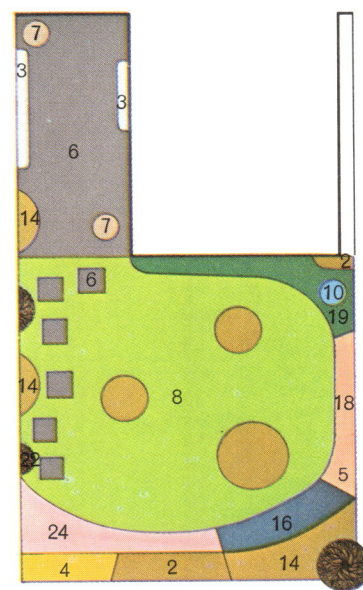

Michael and Angela Harding's garden flourished in spite of an eight-week delay in starting caused by builders. So they began by laying the patio beside their extension; they installed hanging flower-filled baskets and planted earthenware pots with ivy, miniature roses and begonia. Once the rubble had gone, they turned to the garden. They already had two forsythias and a laurel and have added a rhododendron, a maple, a berberis and a cornus (and have ordered a silver conifer for contrast). 'They've done incredibly well,' says Mrs Harding. The new lawn has flourished too, considering they were advised to wait to seed it until the autumn: They abandoned vegetables through lack of space and grew annuals instead.

William James's gardening was interrupted by two lengthy visits to America. His dark garden was not a good situation, so he had some predictable failures – the calendulas, sunflowers and cornflowers did not germinate, the broad beans appeared slowly and then died. Only the French marigolds, gladioli and the standard chrystanthemums (he couldn't find any of the tougher Korean chrysanthemum) survived – and, oddly, the marrows, which love sun. He wisely chose not to attempt a lawn. The brightest spot was his green-stained tub of begonias, geranium and lobelia. Even so, at this stage the rest of the garden was not yet lost: the next six months of the plan concentrated on more permanent and sturdy plants which are better suited to his conditions. He had first made a start by planting eight cuttings of ivy against the sunless south wall.

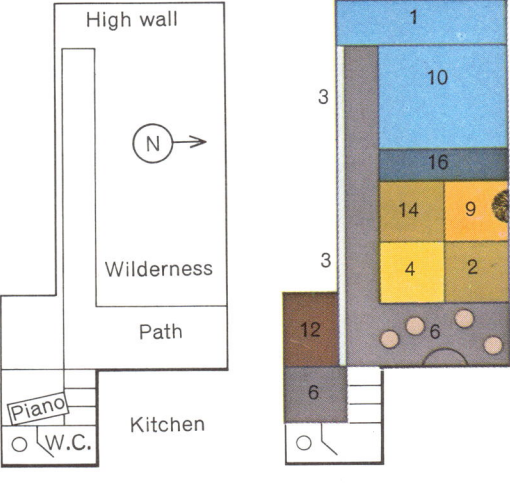

55

Kenneth and Heather MacLeod's garden did not allow for any radical alterations; they already had a patio and an established lawn, so they concentrated on improving what was there. They did not want to remove the trellis, but the morning glory softened its starkness, and when this died the MacLeod's planned to plant a yellow rambling rose. The annual beds curved round the trellis, giving a larger area of colour. This brightness was picked up on the patio by well-filled tubs, a hanging basket and a standard fuschia (instead of a fruit tree). Though they tried all the seeds we recommended, results were disappointing – possibly because they had to fight for space against established shrubs.

They did manage to create a modest vegetable patch and lop a semicircle from the lawn and plant half a dozen runner beans and a herb garden.

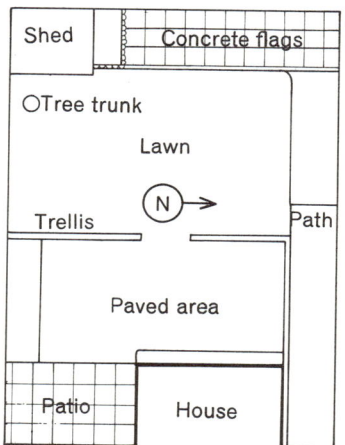 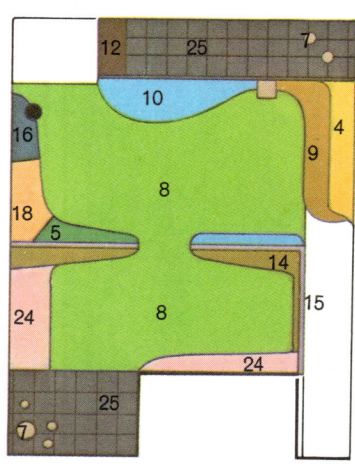

John and Janey Allan could hardly believe after 6 months that their plot of land started off as a jungle; their garden is a striking success story. 'I really enjoy my little rambles round my "estate" first thing in the morning. The Shirley poppies have been a mass of flowers for the last two months – it has taken me a quarter of an hour each morning to dead-head them.' Everything except the morning glory has worked wonderfully; the annual beds are vibrant with colour, ornamental hop covers the left fence, a wall of the garden shed and part of the right fence, the turfed lawn is lush and Janey Allan has already deep-frozen 7 lbs. of carrots and 16 lbs. of beans.

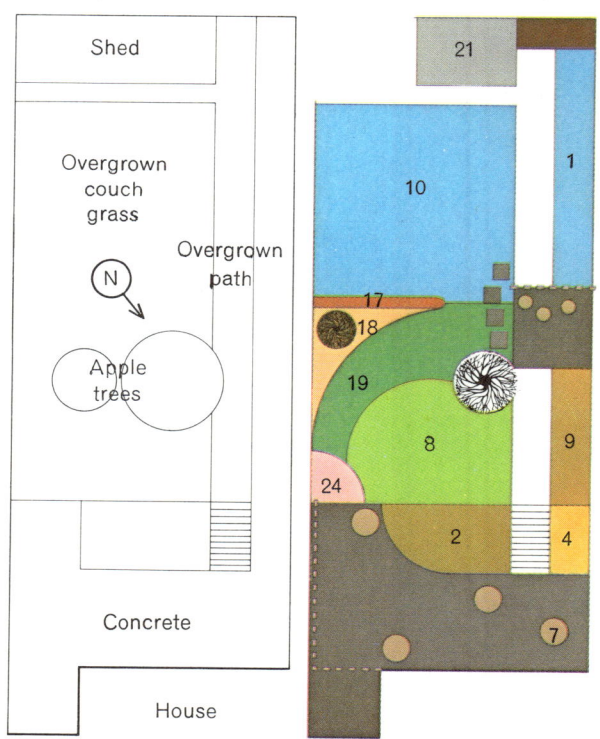

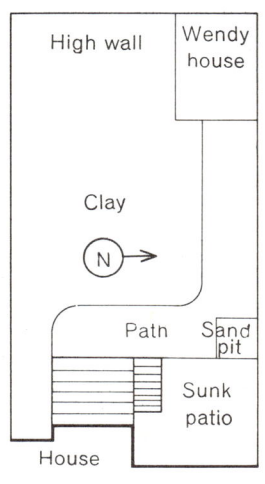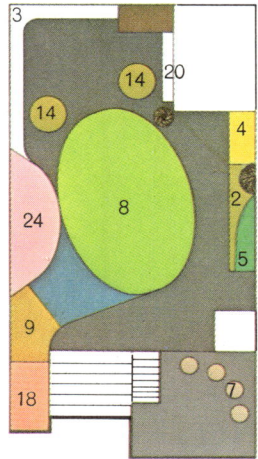

Timothy and Penelope Hicks produced a splendidly elegant town garden in a restricted space. They spent extra time and money in changing the soil. They replaced the top 3 ft. of clay with a lorry load of earth, enriching it with manure and nearly 2 cwt. of peat.

They made two alterations to their original plan – laid crazy paving round the swing and changed the lawn from an oval to a circle. This meant they had more border space on the shady side, so they made a rockery, edging it with a low stone wall.

As only the right-hand side of the garden sees any sun their space for annuals was limited, and there was no room at all for a vegetable patch. Instead they planted two tubs and a stone urn and tomato pots on the patio. On the sunless side, they planted shade lovers.

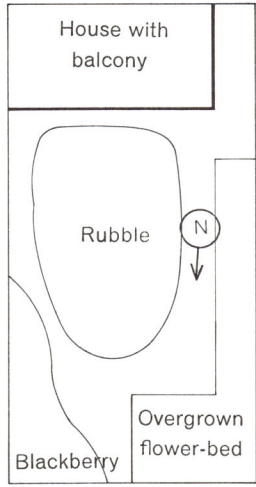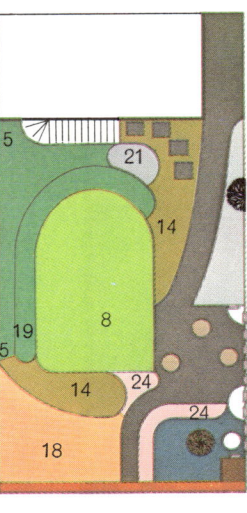

Michael and Jackie Thorpe's garden is the one which, we feel, most closely resembles our artist's impression of how our ideal garden could look after six months – in spite of the not-yet-seeded lawn. The garden itself was an ideal size for our programme, and the Thorpes had to start from scratch – they had no established fixtures to fit in with. Above all, their results have been outstandingly successful, though they have certainly been helped by the fact that the trees do not block the sun, and that their soil was unexpectedly good. One of the most attractive features is the narrow border where they have mixed flowers and decorative vegetables – an edging of alyssum, rows of chilli pepper plants and lettuces and a backing of runner beans.

Stage 14

Bulbs are always great garden favourites, bringing colour at a time of year when most gardens are otherwise dull and cheerless. We plan a blaze of colour near our window with a mixed display bed. Order and purchase now, plant when the annuals have finished flowering and the vegetables have been harvested. Put small bulbs in the cottage garden area or in the lawn to naturalize. Once established they'll spread. Seed grass to complete preparation of new circular lawn.

Needs list: *assortment of mixed bulbs; lawn seed.*
Time budget: *2 hours in 2 weeks*

Flower of the Fortnight

Bulb planting time is here already, and therein lies a lesson: it's just no good rushing out to buy bulbs when everyone else's daffodils are in flower: for a really good show plant August/September. The problem with bulbs, especially for first-time gardeners, is that the choice is bewilderingly wide. Our choice is simple: daffodils, for the whites, saffrons and yellows; tulips in almost every colour except blue; and hyacinths mainly for their scent: go for the blues and pinks for best combined effect. Choose your own varieties from your local garden centre: they'll only sell tried and trusted hardy varieties. Small bulbs offer less colour choice, but extend the bulb season from January through April.

Groundwork

1 Store bulbs waiting to be planted in a cool, dark, dry place. Do not plant them when the ground is wet and sticky. Wait for drier conditions. You do not have to plant your bulbs precisely at midnight on the first night of full moon after September 1 – you've got about a month/6 weeks to plant them. Wait till conditions are right. 2 Check newly planted tree, make sure it is securely tied to its stake, that neither stake nor tie are rubbing bark away. Keep putting lawn clippings/moss peat or compost round base to mulch. 3 Cut lawn less frequently now, and raise the blades on the mower a little. Give the lawn its last feed before it stops growing. 4 Using trowel, dig up any wallflower seedlings and plant in groups among the display bulbs. 5 Watch your gladioli. When all the leaves have died back remove stakes, cut off dead leaves at ground level, store in dry sand or peat in boxes over winter in a dark, frost-free place. 6 Cut chrysanthemum blooms for indoor decoration. 7 Recognize the beetles in your garden: nearly all are beneficial.

Early October weather/soil

A variable month, sometimes cold and wet, sometimes a glowing Indian summer. Can be busy if the weather permits, with the soil still warm enough for planting and plenty of seeds and fruits to harvest. Differences between northern and southern gardens begin to reassert themselves.

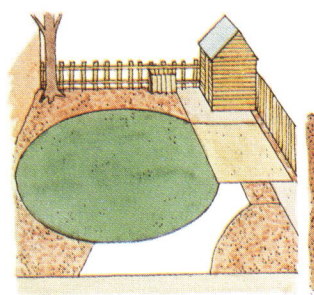 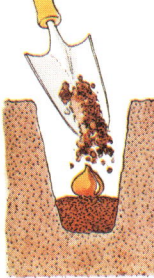 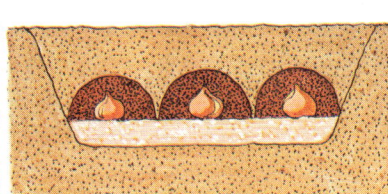 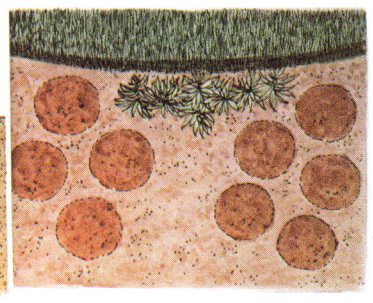

Project work: planting bulbs; collecting seeds; sowing seeds

Spring may still seem a long way off, but now's the time to plant if you want a first rate spring bulb display. First clear the border of annuals and dig up the harvested vegetables. Dig over the bed thoroughly. Add 1 in. layer peat. Rake. Dig bulb holes with trowel. Put handful soilless growing mix in bottom, bed bulbs into it. Top up hole with same mix. On heavy soils, dig circular hole, cover bottom with moss peat/sand/soil, bed bulbs, dome over with soil-less mix, in-fill.

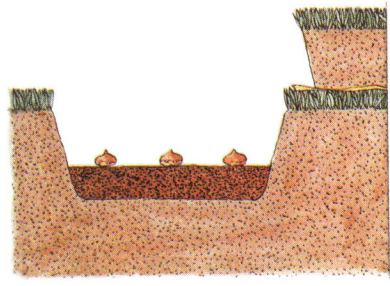  

Crocuses are excellent under grass. Look natural. Lift turf (Stage 8), prepare hole as shown, plant as for other bulbs, replace turf, refirm.

Chionodoxa, crocus, bluebell, snowdrop, are all bulbs suitable for naturalizing by planting as for crocus. Collect heads of 1 Shirley poppy, 2 calendula, place heads in separate envelopes, label. Sow seed next spring. Seeds store best in a cool, dry, dark cupboard.

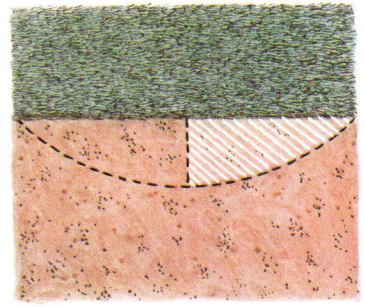 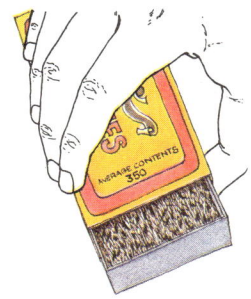 

Move to ground prepared in Stage 12 for new lawn. Soil will have settled. Remove weeds, rake lightly and level. Mark out into areas 1 yd^2.

Buy general purpose lawn seed. Put 2 oz. in a matchbox. Scatter over 1 yd^2. Do not exceed this rate. Repeat process over next square yard.

Rake seed into soil lightly drawing towards you with one hand while scattering sand over the seed with the other hand. Do not water.

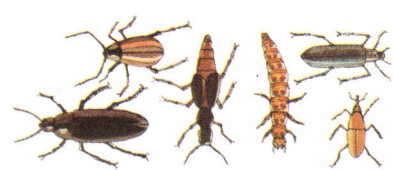

Stage 15

Needs list: *trellis materials; 3 pressure-treated softwood posts 7 ft 6 in long; nine battens 4 ft 6 in long; six battens 2 ft long – all 2 in by 1 ft; expanding (or rigid) softwood trellis; about 6 in mesh, 3 panels 4 ft 6 in by 5 ft; 1 pkt 2 in brass screws; 1 gal creosote; 1 28 lb bag cement/sand mix; 4 pieces old pipe 2 ft long; 1 climbing rose; 1 clematis plant.*

Time budget: *8 hours in 2 weeks*

A trellis is an essential if you want to grow some of the most exciting climbing plants – roses, clematis, things like that. Don't skimp on construction. Any plant growing well will soon get heavy enough to pull a flimsy trellis down. So build it really solidly. We show the construction of a wooden trellis, but you can use plastic covered mesh if you prefer. The fall brings a busy harvest time in the vegetable plot and from any fruit trees or bushes.

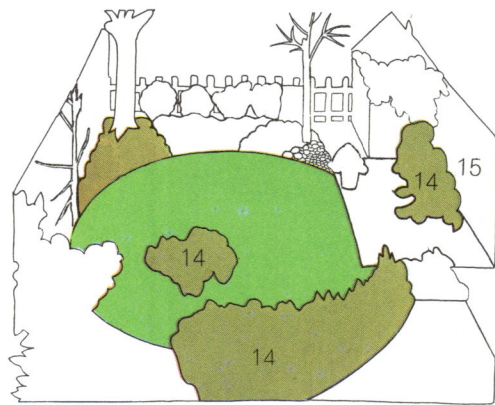

Flower of the Fortnight

Traditionally roses are everyone's favourite plant: certainly in Britain they outsell all other woody plants by something like ten to one. Many people will tell you, 'If you haven't got roses, you haven't got a garden'. In a small space garden optimize your wall space: go for climbing roses. These flower prolifically on young wood growing from an old wood framework. Rambling roses grow from the base every year. Both are suitable. Literally hundreds of varieties are available: some of the best are 'Handel', 'Golden Showers', 'Parkdirektor Riggers', all climbers; 'Dorothy Perkins', 'Félicité et Perpétue' (ramblers). Check your local garden centre for varieties for your area.

Groundwork

You're right in the harvesting season now for most vegetables. Pole beans will keep producing till first frost. Don't wait for other vegetables to grow too big. Most taste best if you pick them when they are two-thirds the size the catalogues say they'll grow to. Carrots, radishes, lettuces are typically tastier if picked young. Keep picking beans and they'll keep on producing. If you manage to crop more tomatoes than you can eat at once, pickle the surplus ones. Salt down or deep freeze surplus beans. Don't harvest potatoes till the haulms (tops) have died right down. Put all vegetable waste in the compost bin, including spent plants. Material at the bottom of the bin should be peaty and odourless by now. Dig it out, use it as a mulch, turn the rest, keep adding to the top. Even better, start a second bin once the first is full. Use them alternate years. Gives best results in the end. If you're getting interested in which bugs are friends and which are foes, borrow books from your local library, read up on the subject.

Mid October weather/soil

Autumn's giving way to winter, stripping the last leaves off the trees. Day/night length roughly equal, starts many plants into dormancy: day length matters here as much as temperature. But already the garden is starting on its way to next year's flowers, with bulbs swelling underground.

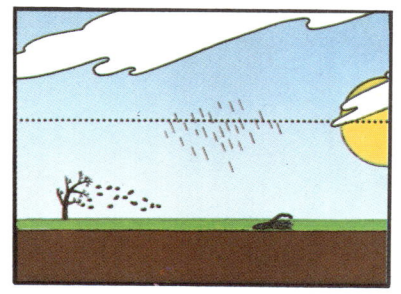

Project work: erecting trellis, planting vines

The trellis you make now will be a permanent asset not only to your garden but to your property and its value – provided you make it well. So make it well, and it will serve you well. No skimping or short-cuts here please. First, dig your post holes at least 2 ft deep. Ours are 4 ft. 6 in. apart – a spacing we suggest you follow. Put crocks in the bottom of the hole. Stand 1 non-glazed clay land drain pipe upright in the bottom of each hole. Next creosote the part of the post that will be in the ground. Hammer in thick nails all round the part to be buried. Insert prepared poles one by one into the upright land-drain pipes in the holes. Check that all posts are vertical from all directions: use spirit level, plumb line. Wedge the post in its pipe, and the pipe in its hole, using rubble. Nail temporary struts from fence to hold post in position. Prepare strong cement/sand mix, pour into pipe and into hole round pipe. Tamp down, top up, tamp again, level off, leaving the cement/sand mix slightly shouldered up against the post as a watershed. Leave 1 week to set. Creosote posts. Then fit horizontal battens, 3 per bay, each 4 ft. 6 in. long. Countersink battens into posts if you can: looks better, lasts longer. Fix battens to posts with 2 in. screws. Fix trellis panels to battens using ½ in. screws. If using a plastic-covered wire trellis fix to the battens with heavy duty plastic-coated wire. Finally, as an optional extra, cap the trellis: sheds rain, keeps trellis in good shape longer. If you're putting the trellis on the shed, don't use posts, start at the battens stage. Plant a rose at the foot of one post, a honeysuckle at the foot of one post, a wisteria at the foot of another, and *Clematis montana* or its pink form at the foot of the third, always planting into a well-prepared hole. Keep neat for best effect. Only re-creosote the trellis when the plants are dormant. Creosote on the leaves can kill.

Stage 16

Your garden is only as good as the soil in it. Successful gardening comes from fertile soil in good heart, regularly replenished with humus and plant foods. You can make any soil good soil if you work on it. Find out about your local soil from your local garden club or newspaper gardening column. We help you discover the personality type of the soil in your backyard. And we continue with our permanent planting programme, this fortnight with lavender and candytuft.

Needs list: *5 lavender plants; 7 Iberis plants; ½ cwt/50 lb bag moss peat.*
Time budget: *3 hours in 1 week*

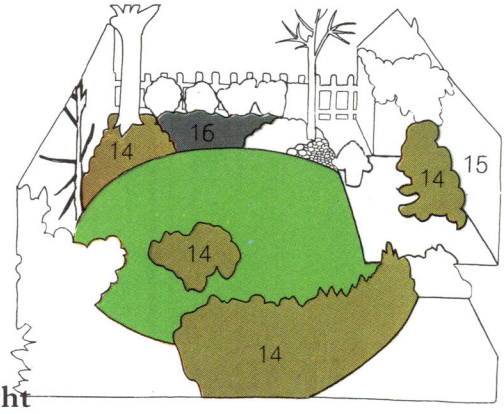

Flower of the Fortnight

This fortnight's flower is a plant of many qualities: grown primarily for its scent, it has pretty spikes of lavender flowers, delightful grey foliage, which contrasts well with the prevalent greens of other plants and stays on the plant through winter, it also makes first rate ground cover, keeping down all the weeds under it. There are many varieties of lavender around, tall, dwarf, some lighter, some darker in flower: there's even a pink one! The one we've chosen is lavender 'Hidcote' – the richest coloured form of all. Either cut the flowers just as they open to dry for making sachets, or leave them on and let the plant seed. Give full sun, sharp drainage and clip back each spring to keep tidy.

Groundwork

1 Your newly seeded lawn should be ready now for its first mow. Should be about 3 in. high. Set mower blades as high as they'll go. Mow lightly. Do not pull the grass, don't skid the mower on it. Still keep kids and pets off it. 2 Plant daffodils this month: they need a head start on other bulbs. Tulips, hyacinths and small bulbs like snowdrops, crocuses, can wait till next month. 3 Rake up leaves from lawn and cottage garden area. Put them in the compost bin. Do not add any more fertilizer to the lawn till spring. Keep the surface free of weeds. Rake out moss if it's a problem. Scatter worm casts when they appear, but don't try to kill the worms: they help the lawn grow well. 4 Dig over the area where the beans were growing, and plant flowers there following the instructions given in Stage 5. Plant in staggered rows. Soak well. Use spare time to read up about climate, soil. Find out rainfall for your area, soil type, the average date of the first and last killing frost = $32°F/0°C$. Allow for altitude if you live on a hilltop.

Early November weather/soil

Gardens and gardeners alike are now just about in full hibernation. However, the soil is still warmer now than in January or February, so hardy shrubs and trees can still be planted when the soil's workable. Protect roots of shrubs/trees waiting to be planted with leaves or peat.

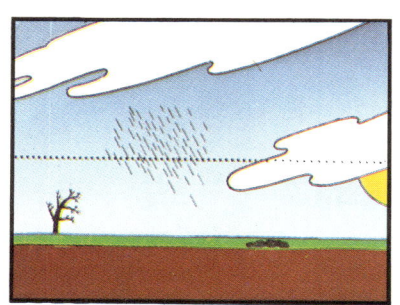

Project work: soil; what is it?

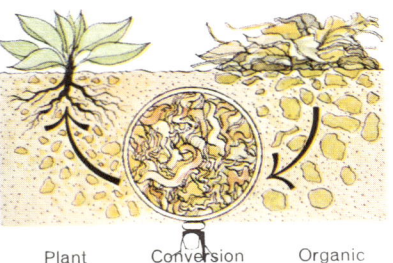
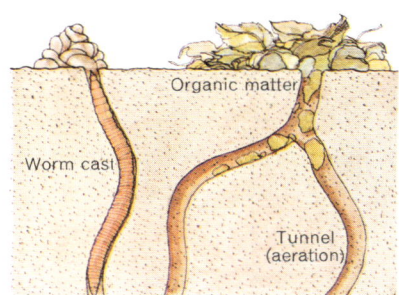
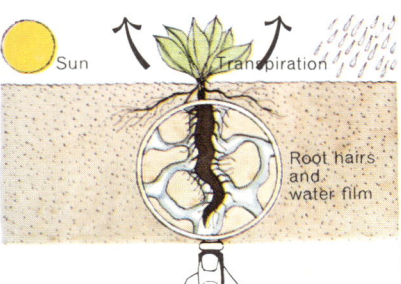
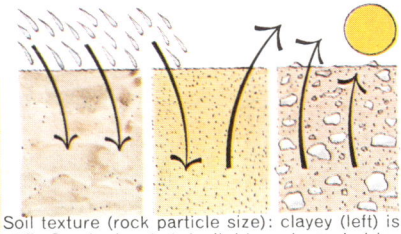

Soil texture (rock particle size): clayey (left) is stiff. Sandy (centre) is light, wets and dries easily. Stony (right) is difficult.

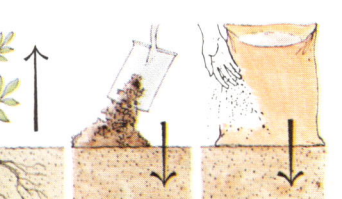

Plants take mineral salts. Composts feed soil creatures. They and fertilisers replace mineral salts. The cycle is complete.

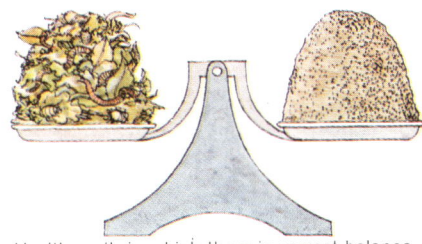

Healthy soil: in which there is correct balance between creatures, rock particles (texture) and mineral salts. Example: rich, loamy soil.

Rhododendron (left) needs an acid soil; Wayfaring tree (right) prefers an alkaline one. Most plants (centre) grow in in-between soil.

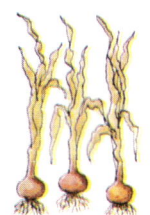

Most people think of soil as a sort of inert, brownish something or other out of which plants stick. To master your garden, to make the plants in it thrive with the least effort on your part, you need to know a lot more about soil than that. Take a handful of soil from your garden and contemplate it. It's made up of 5 things: (a) mineral particles which have been formed by the erosion of mountains over eons; the type of rock they came from will be the main factor that determines whether your soil is acid or alkaline; the size of the particles will determine whether you have clay, good loam, light sand or just plain stony soil. (b) Organic matter, known as humus, which acts as a sponge and holds water between the mineral particles. (c) Soil life – myriads of teeming creatures, mainly microscopic, but some quite large, like earthworms. One boffin estimated that there are 100,000 micro-organisms in every cubic centimeter of good loam. They convert humus into the mineral salts plant need to feed on. Earthworms pull fallen leaves &c. down into soil. All part of the process. (d) Air: plant roots need air to breathe. (e) Water. Plant roots must have water since they can only absorb essential plant foods in solution. Whether your soil is good, bad or horrible is mainly a matter of the proportions of mineral particles to humus. Extremes are pure peat, which will grow practically nothing since there is no air in it; and pure sand, which won't grow much either because it has no humus. Add sand and compost to peat soils to make them good, and peat and compost to any other soil type to improve it. The more humus = moss peat/compost/&c. you add, the more soil micro-organisms there'll be to convert the humus into plant foods, especially the vital 3, N, P, K = nitrogen, phosphorus, potassium. Acidity is another key factor, limiting the types of plants you can grow, Buy a soil testing kit.

Stage 17

Use your sunny walls and fences to best effect – our slogan for all gardeners. Planting fan-trained fruit trees will involve a real test of your new gardening skills. Fruits like apples and pears need other varieties nearby to ensure good pollination and fruiting, so unless your neighbours grow these fruits too, choose instead a peach, apricot, nectarine or plum. We screen our far boundary with a hedge, and take another good look at improving our soil.

Needs list: *1 fan-trained fruit tree; 4 Cotoneaster simonsii; 1 coil medium gauge wire.*
Time budget: *5 hours in 2 weeks*

Mid November weather/soil

Dormant season for most plants: nurseries despatch most stock now. Plant when soil is not frozen, not waterlogged. Often a wet month, so note parts of the garden where water collects; make plans to drain them. Badly drained soils can kill plants which would thrive otherwise.

Flower of the Fortnight

There's an old saying that you plant pears for your heirs. Forget it. With modern dwarfing rootstocks and newer fan-training techniques you can be sure of fruits after only a few years. The pear we illustrate is the world famous 'Conference', one of the hardiest, most adaptable and, what's more, partly self-fertile. You need cross pollination for heavy fruiting, so plant 'Packham's Triumph' or 'William's' to ensure success. Fan train as shown. In really warm, sheltered gardens, try a peach, apricot or nectarine against the sunniest wall in the garden. If you've only got a wall in shade all the time, grow a sour cherry. Keep it fan-trained flat against the wall. Tie in straggly branches.

Groundwork

Check supplies bought in, make sure you have adequate supplies for winter. Moss peat: 2 cwt. (Stages 2, 4, 11, 16). Make sure enough remains for digging over beds. Buy more if needed. Bonemeal: 1 pkt. (Stages 2, 5). Make final application now, around established plants, 4 oz. per yd^2. Lawn fertilizer: 1 pkt. (Stage 5). Make last application Stage 15. Start again when grass is growing vigorously in spring. Liquid plant feed: 1 bottle (Stage 7). For container and indoor plants. Latter are now dormant. Do not feed again until new growth starts next year. Growing mix: 1 bag (Stage 7). Store, or use for indoor bulbs, plants. Farmyard manure: 1 bag (Stage 9). Mulch round base of fan-trained fruit trees, climbing/rambler roses. Find or create suitable storage space in shed, garage, crawl-space. Must be dry, cool, secure. Make sure all chemicals – artificial fertilizers, weedkillers, pesticides, insecticides – are out of reach of children, preferably in a locked cupboard. Never transfer chemicals into other containers. Use garage to store bulky materials.

Project work: a fruit tree against a wall; improving your soil

Select the type of fruit you want to grow in your garden: consider all aspects – suitability of climate, soil and position in garden. Then choose a pre-trained tree of the type best suited to your garden – espalier, fan, cordon. The choice is yours. Purchase. Fix ties before planting. To fix ties, use staples (Stage 3) and wire: make sure wire is taut between staples. Use tighteners if necessary. Soak the roots of the tree in a pail of water for 1 night before planting. To plant, lift turf, dig a pit 2 ft. deep, and at least 18 in. across from wall to outer edge of hole, put 6 in. layer of rubble/bricks/stones at the bottom of the hole. Make a soilless growing mix heap at the bottom of the hole. Place fruit tree on that and spread the roots away from the wall. Backfill, leaving a length of hose or something similar in position close to the stem (allow room for stem to grow) for irrigation in future. Firm. Soak. Tie in branches to wires with twine. Mulch with compost. Next plant *Cotoneaster simonsii* along fence. Prepare planting holes as described in other stages, and space the plants 2 ft. apart 18 in. from the fence. Next set about improving your soil. Peat is the key soil improver, a miracle-worker for tired, dusty soils. Dig over any empty ground, adding a 1 in. layer of peat and incorporating it in the top 6 in. of soil as you dig. Just keep on using it all the time. Use moss peat for mulches, to suppress weeds, use it every time you plant. Peat makes your soil spongier, more moisture retentive, but it doesn't feed the soil. So in addition use organic fertilizers – compost, farmyard manure, whatever is available. Seaweed, shoddy, sewer sludge all feed the soil. Find out what is easiest to obtain in your area. For pot-plants use soilless growing mix: give additional feeds with foliar feeds through the leaves. Tip used soilless mixes from pots, tubs, containers on to borders too.

Stage 18

The fall is rapidly giving way to winter, and that can be an exciting time for gardeners – a time for browsing through catalogues and round garden centres. Look particularly for shrubs, they're a great investment. Don't buy everything in sight: check eventual height and spread: check hardiness suitability for your area; check soil suitability too. Our choice is suitable for most gardens in most areas. Check with a local nurseryman if in doubt.

Needs list: *6 assorted flowering shrubs.*
Time budget: *5 hours in 2 weeks*

Flower of the Fortnight

Hypericum patulum, St. John's wort, is ideal for modern small gardens. Of compact habit, reaching only 3 or 4 ft., it bears huge rich golden yellow flowers from high summer through late fall. These are followed by bright red fruits. It's semi-evergreen, only loosing its leaves in hard winters. It thrives in almost any soil (not waterlogged ones) and does well in poor soils. All the attention it needs is a light pruning in spring, just clipping back old flowering shoots and weak wood.

Groundwork

Cut down your dahlias to within 4 in. of the base. Lift them carefully from the soil, taking care not to damage the tubers; like don't stick the lifting fork through them. Leave tubers to dry in a cool, airy place for 2 weeks, then rub the mud off. Check each tuber to make sure it is firm. Throw away any that are mushy. Store firm tubers in a tray packed in dry moss peat, leaving the crown of each tuber above the peat. Keep them in a cool, dry, dark, frost-free place till spring. Clean and store support stakes and/or canes. Cut dead chrysanthemum tops off to 1 in. from ground level. Leave in the ground over winter. Meet the last in our list of garden friends. (1) the Ichneumon fly – a delicate, lacy bug – and a parasite on caterpillars. Does good work keeping caterpillar population down. (2) the caddis fly; its larvae feed on aphids. Never destroy these two thinking they're enemies. If you've just sown a lawn don't water it: it'll pan the soil. Time to clean up the mower, grease it, put it in storage for the winter.

Late November weather/soil

Frosts should be hitting hard in northern districts by now, but may not have reached southern districts yet. A good time to catch up on construction work if you've got behind – patio, trellis, drainage – things like that. Heavy snow can crush many plants, snap boughs. Shake it off branches.

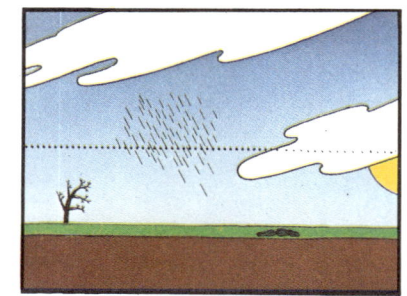

Project work; a selection of shrubs; rockery/rock garden stone collecting

Shrubs have a place in every garden. Use them with care, as accent plants here and there, not everywhere. A garden full of shrubs and nothing else is dull for 9 months out of every 12. A garden needs plants of every type – shrubs, trees, annuals, biennials, perennials, bulbs – the lot. Shrubs offer the widest range; plant them for flower, fruit, autumn colour, because they grow narrowly upright or because they sprawl across the ground. Buy them for their berries or their coloured leaves. Most shrubs come in containers these days. Store in shaded, sheltered place if the ground is frozen or too wet to plant in – as for tree (Stage 13). Prepare hole 2 ft. across 18 in. deep, make a mound of soilless growing mix, remove shrub from container, position on growing mix dome, backfill with same mix, firming every 3 or 4 in. Finally firm, soak, mulch. Prune any broken twigs. *Berberis thunbergii* (1) has bright orange flowers, good autumn colour. *Berberis thunbergii atropurpurea* (2) same plus bronze leaves – a favourite with flower arrangers. *Chaenomeles* 'Rowallane' (3) red flowers before leaves in spring, yellow fruits, good against a wall, leggy, spready in the open. *Mahonia aquifolium* (4) evergreen leaves of fine, sculptural shape, turn crimson through winter, yellow flowers, winter, blue fruits spring. *Viburnum opulus* 'Compactum' (5) white flowers, showy red berries, compact. Dwarf evergreen azaleas (6), rhododendrons (7) and camellias (not shown) strictly for acid soils. See if your neighbours grow them. Or grow in containers filled with peat only. Spacing: check catalogues for ultimate size. Plant so branches will meet, tallest at back of border, smallest at the front. Next think ahead to your rockery/rock garden. Keep your eyes open. Collect interesting stone, pieces of masonry, moulding from demolition sites rocks from quarries, hillsides.

Stage 19

There's a whole galaxy of colourful plants available today among the herbaceous perennials. The roots you buy may seem small, but month by month, year by year, they grow into clumps of hardy, trouble-free flowers. You can increase them yourself. Having examined our soil a couple of stages back, we now take a closer look at pesticides. Our final contribution to the cottage garden perennial patch is the Christmas rose which we plant 18 in./46 cm. from the colchicums.

Needs list: *3 Christmas rose plants; 16 herbaceous perennials.*
Time budget: *5 hours in 3 weeks*

Flower of the Fortnight

The Christmas rose (*Helleborus niger*) is a marvellous little tufted perennial plant with much-divided leaves and huge white flowers borne right in mid-winter. Grow it in rich, dampish soil in shade. Once planted, never move it. Protect flowers from frost with a pane of glass on stilts.

Groundwork

The first thing to deal with now are your container-grown plants. Pelargoniums and fuchsias can be overwintered in their pots (Stage 7). Prune dead stems of all remaining flowers. Keep dormant plants in a frost-free shed, garage, crawl-space or the like: if you bring them indoors and put them on a window-sill keep them out of direct sunlight otherwise they will start growing again. Also keep them cool. Keep the soil almost but not quite dry. Good light and warmth will keep the plants growing, which could kill them. Start keeping records, planning ahead. Make a chart on your garden chemicals cupboard: record chores and when they need to be done, plants that need a special watch kept on them for bugs; record when to plant corms (e.g. gladioli) – tubers (e.g. dahlias); you don't always remember from one year till the next. Also note anything you should have done but have not had time to do. A garden never stands still: you can't afford to either. Learn to work with your garden, encourage plants that do well: don't fight nature.

Early December weather/soil

December can be a stormy month with heavy rains and increasingly severe frosts. Grab the chance to garden when you can: little point in planning. Work on the patio can go ahead, but watch weather forecasts and protect new-laid concrete/cement with sacking when frosts threaten.

Project work: 8 kinds of herbaceous perennials; bug hunting

The eight herbaceous perennials shown here are some of the finest of all garden plants, flowering for months on end. All are hardy, reliable and first-rate performers. Buy plants when they are dormant from your local garden centre. Store in a cool, shaded place as for tree (Stage 13). Prepare bed, digging thoroughly, picking out weeds, roots, stones. Add 1 in. layer of moss peat, dig in lightly, sprinkle bone meal. Leave. Re-position Korean chrysanthemum before planting perennials if you want to: also wallflowers (which die after flowering). Space according to size, tallest at back, smallest in front.

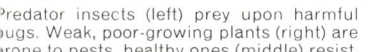

Predator insects (left) prey upon harmful bugs. Weak, poor-growing plants (right) are prone to pests, healthy ones (middle) resist. Thrush keeps surplus worms down, bee pollinates blossom, violet ground beetle attacks slug: parts of the wildlife cycle. Get to know all creatures.

A healthy plant in a healthy soil is far less likely to be afflicted with pests and diseases than an unhealthy plant growing in poor soil. Moral: all that work you put in digging moss peat into the soil pays off more ways than one. It encourages a healthy insect population, counterbalanced by natural insect enemies. Only act against bugs when essential.

Pesticides: from herbal brews (left) to chemicals (right); cigarette butts (nicotine) detergent (Stage 3) in water, amateur ways. Soils, plants, and animals are harmed by: cropping without replacing depleted plant foods, indiscriminate use of pesticides.

If you have to take action against bugs, don't reach for the ultimate aerosol of chemical killer at once. Move by stages. Stage 1: a strong jet of water will knock most bugs off plants: many will not come back for more. Stage 2: Use soapy water (see back to Stage 3). Stage 3: pyrethrum, a vegetable extract. Usually effective. Don't use on chrysanthemums Stage 4: use Derris.

Stage 20

We take time off to tell you about tubs. Maybe you'll use them next year – it's too late for this year, or maybe you had the sense to look ahead and find this page earlier. The time to plant tubs is when you put your bedding plants out. Trouble is, we've been so busy telling you many other things that will improve your garden once and forever, that this little item got left aside. After all, you have to replant your tubs every year. But the effect is stunning.

Needs list: *1 plant container (preferably unvarnished tub); three 4 ft canes; 1 bag growing mix; 1 bottle liquid plant feed; 1 pelargonium or 1 fuchsia; 4 trailing lobelia; 6 summer bedding begonia; 1 bellflower.*
Time budget: *4 hours in 2 weeks*

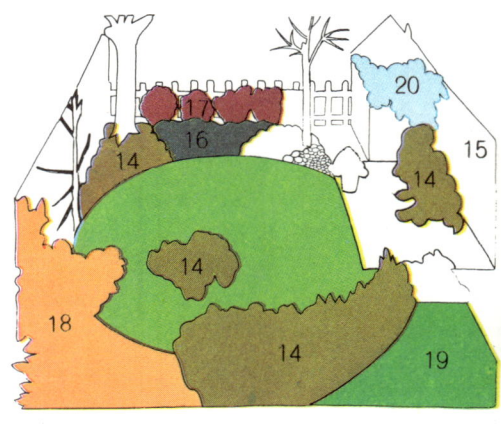

Mid December weather/soil

The shortest day of the year arrives before Christmas, and gardeners can take new heart as they start to see the days grow longer. The rawness of December weather keeps most gardeners indoors, giving them a good opportunity to catch up on homework, learning about bugs, weeds.

Flower of the Fortnight

The spring star flower (*Ipheion uniflora*) is either the most desirable of spring flowers or the most detestable of spring weeds depending on how much you like it and how much it likes you. Growing no more than 9 in. high, tufts of narrow strap-shaped blue-green leaves spring from white bulbs. Held high above these are the beautifully shaped blue star-like flowers, each with a white stripe down the middle of every petal. 'Wisley Blue' is much bluer than the common type, and there is a lovely pure white form as well. It needs a sunny place and well-drained soil. If it likes you it will seed everywhere, so plant it where it can naturalize. Bulbs have long tap roots and are hard to eradicate.

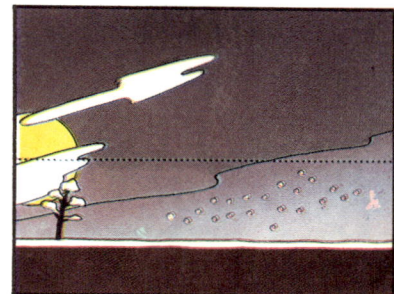

Groundwork

Here are some suggestions for improving and feeding your soil. Relate your soil improvement and feeding programme to what you learned about your soil in Stages 16 and 17. Top-dressing: these are plant foods you scatter on the surface of the soil; apply spring and autumn. Artificial fertilizers must be raked in. General purpose fertilizers: get one bag organic fertilizer containing a suitable NPK ratio for your soil; usually a dehydrated animal or poultry manure. Top dress the soil: the slow-release nutrients will become available to the plants over a long period. Or use bone meal. Vegetables: one 28 lb. bag inorganic fertilizer, quick-acting. Top dress fortnightly spring through mid summer. Or use fish meal. Or liquid feed crops. Do not use all three. Heavy clay: 1 bag soil conditioner, which helps break down the structure of heavy clays, makes them more friable, easier to work, easier for plants to grow in. Acid soils, tired down soils: top dress with garden lime every 2 years; $\frac{1}{2}$ lb. per yd^2. Don't overdo the lime if you want to grow acid-loving plants.

Project work: planting up a container; and elementary soil testing

Containers give you a chance to grow plants that otherwise you probably wouldn't grow. Most of them are tender (plants that would be killed by frost), and all of them very very colourful. This is the best way of achieving a splash of colour on the patio. Take a container – a half barrel, a tub, even a wooden box – and make sure that it has plenty of drainage holes in the bottom. Place it on the patio. Raise it off the ground by setting four bricks under it. If you don't do this all sorts of bugs – earwigs, lice and so on, will get into your container and feast on the roots of your precious plants. Cover the bottom of the container with 3 in. crocks, broken roof tiles, large pebbles for drainage. Half fill with soilless growing mix. Keep pelargoniums and fuchsias in their pots, and place the pots so that their rims are 1 in. below the rim of the container. In-fill with soilless growing mix till this is level with the tops of the pots. Push in three 4 ft. canes round the centre pot. Plant 2 peat pots of home-grown seedlings of nasturtiums and/or Canary creeper at the foot of each cane. Lace twine round canes for these to climb – see illustration. Plant bedding begonias hard up against the peat pots containing the nasturtiums/Canary creeper. Plant blue lobelia and white bellflowers alternately round the edges. They will trail over the sides and largely hide the tub. Make all plants firm, then soak thoroughly. Never let the planting dry out. Next, move some house pot plants outside. Here's how to succeed with them. Take the plants, still in their pots, and put them into a container about twice the size of the one they're growing in. Fill the gap between the inner and the outer container with soilless growing mix. Next test your soil, see what its made of. Stir 2 tbsp garden soil into 1 jar tap water. Check against the illustrations to see which type you have. Keep improving it with moss peat.

Stage 21

With Christmas coming up, it's time to remember that plants make lovely presents. Trouble is, many people find their flowers beginning to fade all too soon, so we give some tips on keeping these plants healthy. Garden centres and florists will have a wide and exciting range of plants available – but read the labels and instructions carefully, and don't send difficult plants to people who aren't greenthumbs. We also tell you about a fly-deterrent kitchen pot plant.

Needs list: *Christmas present plants; 1 pkt mignonette seed; 1 pkt 3 in peat pots.*
Time budget: *7 hours in 2 weeks*

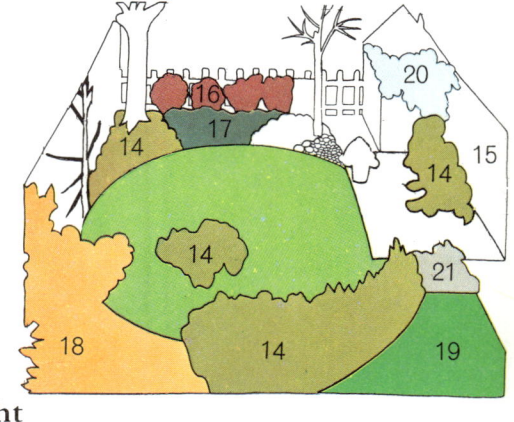

Flower of the Fortnight

Round about Christmas time every florist's shop and garden centre in sight will be full of houseplant cyclamen – a glorious array of colour, every shade of pink from purest white through to scarlets, crimsons and purples, some with bi-coloured flowers, with petals fringed, fluted, spirally twisted, and many with marvellous leaf markings. Buy plants with lots of buds but few flowers open. Give them a cool, well-lit position. When watering, soak the plants, then let them dry out before watering again. Never splash water over the corm: it could rot it. After flowering let leaves turn yellow, dry corm completely, then start into growth by watering around July for Christmas flowering.

Groundwork

Now summer's leaves have fallen, been swept up and put in the compost bin, and winter's setting in, its time to check up on routine maintenance chores around the garden. Repair damaged fences as soon as you notice damage: don't wait till later. They deteriorate very quickly once damaged. Repair mortar in walls, especially behind newly planted fan-trained trees. Check trellis and other construction work, to see it's still stable, safe. Keep patio construction work under burlap/sacking in frosty weather. If you take the nurseryman's or garden centre labels off plants, keep a record of what you planted where. If you get enthusiastic, make a grid of your garden and keep a card index of what you planted in which segment. Learn the Latin names of the plants. Common names are often confusing. If you're given a plant as a present and it looks a bit jaded, put it in a light room with an even temperature. Avoid rooms that are too hot, too stuffy, too dark, too dry. Create atmospheric humidity round the plant, see picture of cyclamen opposite.

Late December weather/soil

Cold, wet soil just as much as cold, damp air and low night temperatures severely restrict gardening now. Plants stay firmly underground or dormant. Statistically this is the coldest month of the year. Time to stay indoors and learn about new techniques, such as pruning.

Project work: plants indoors; ivy tubs and a living fly-repellent

Winter is quite definitely the time for indoor gardening: just one thing: if you start indoor gardening in winter, don't forget the plants in summer – it's all too easily done. Rule 1 for just about all house plants – except cacti, succulents – is that they like atmospheric humidity. More plants are killed in homes because the air in homes is centrally heated and dry than any other way. Here's how to beat the problem. Take a bowl about twice the diameter of the pot. Place pebbles in the bottom. Place the pot on the pebbles. Keep water at the bottom of the bowl in among the pebbles. Be sure the water level never reaches the bottom of the pot. Next grow your own herbs. Start seeds in peat pots filled with soilless growing mix. Plant out late spring/early summer – 4 weeks after your last official frost. On your patio, move your tub/container to a sunny, sheltered spot. Plant up with fancy-leaved ivies to trail over the edge. Use reference books to identify plant presents you've been given.

The Mignonette. Mignonette is one of the most delightful of all the old-fashioned flowers, and has been treasured for centuries for its sweetly scented flowers. The flowers are not as bright as those of many modern plants, which is probably why it is less widely grown now than it used to be. In a drab, busy world we want gay, garish colours in our gardens. We're growing mignonette not as a garden plant, but as a house plant, for the kitchen. Reason? Its marvellous scent repels flies. Sow seed in peat pots filled with a soilless growing mix, thin seedlings to 3 plants per pot. Place peat pot in a crocked clay pot of slightly larger diameter, fill gap with soilless growing mix. Stand in ornamental plant container on kitchen window sill. Give spares to friends. If you've still got spares to spare plant them in the garden.

Stage 22

In the dead, dull days of winter it's time to take a look at house plants, and think about decoration in the garden. Many plants, indoors and out, can be increased by cuttings, and now's a good time to learn about that. Our ice plant, for the base of the flowering crab, dies back in winter, which is when the painted stones come into their own, bringing colour to the garden when otherwise there might be none. We also give you tips on a rockery that will look great.

Needs list: *3 aubretia plants.*
Time budget: *3 hours in 2 weeks*

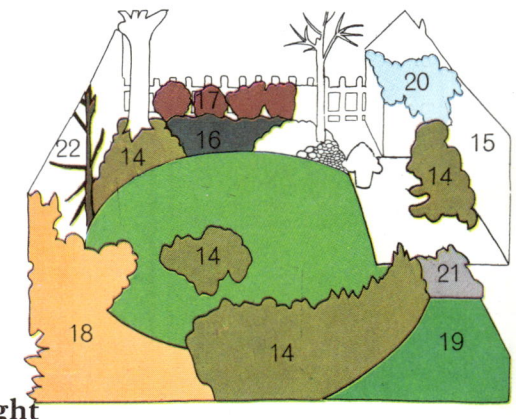

Flower of the Fortnight

Bulbs in bowls always fascinate. You can have them in flower in bowls weeks before they'd be in flower in the garden. *Iris danfordiae* (illustrated), crocuses, snowdrops, scillas can all be forced. Pot up the bulbs September/October in bulb fibre that is just damp – not wet. In undrained bowls put some charcoal in the bottom. Put the bowl somewhere cool, damp and dark, cellar, crawl-space or outdoors under a pile of cinders in shade. On 1 December move the bulbs into a little light and a slightly warmer place. Gradually increase light and warmth. Once leaves are up and green and the buds are showing, give full light and more warmth. Keep bulb fibre damp. After flowering, discard bulbs.

January weather/soil

Grey leaden skies and earth hard as iron typify February, but the warmth of the sun when it does come through hints at spring to come. With longer days to tempt one outside, a good time to make a start on the rockery, and to take a look at house plants and to learn to take cuttings.

Groundwork

Rockery/rock garden: if the rocks you collect are heavy and cumbersome, sling them into position by using a pair of straps to suspend the rock from a pole. It takes two of you to move it. Allow the natural gravity of the rock to determine the way it lies. On the inner face of the rockery small stones can be used as wedges to give greater stability to wobbly rocks. The construction of a solid-looking rock face can be extended as the supply of materials and time allows. Completed face can be planted up. Try to imitate a natural rock outcrop: A heap of rocks chucked on a pile of earth does not make a rockery/rock garden. Mix coarse grit with a soil-based growing mix for your rock plants to ensure perfect drainage. Cover the surface of the rockery with coarse grit: looks good, forms a natural mulch to keep weeds down and keep the growing mix moist while the heads of the plants are in sun, which is what most rock plants like. Time now to start looking out for honesty seedlings (below right). Don't transplant these until the spring.

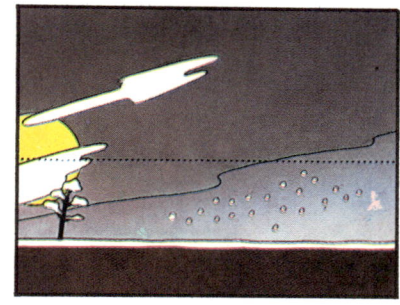

Project work: easy house plants; cuttings

If you're going to grow house plants start with some easy ones. Tradescantia (top left) and zebrina are similar; both have a loose, trailing way of growing; the latter can be distinguished by its glistening leaves. The spider plant (top right) looks rather like grass, broad green and white variegated leaves, growing in a tuft. Sends up long wands, tiny white flowers on the ends which droop and sprout new plants. Layer plantlets into fresh pots, hold firm with a hairpin. Learn about cuttings. Many, like ivies, busy Lizzies, fuchsias will root easily in water or soilless seed mix with extra sand; take 6 in. cuttings from tips of branches in high summer. Dip cut end in hormone rooting powder: tap off surplus: plant. Keep moist. Make yourself a bottle garden – the ideal way to grow plants indoors: put ½ in. charcoal over bottom, 1 in. coarse grit, 2 in. soilless growing mix. Landscape with rocks. Plant ferns, tradescantias, African violets &c. Use your ingenuity to create unexpected garden features; plant a chimney stack with ivies, trailing pelargoniums or similar. Landscape a stone sink with rocks, plant up with dwarf conifers, heathers, bulbs &c. Or buy a broken storm drain (round or square) from a builder's merchant and plant up similarly. Get that rockery/rock garden moving: a long-term project, don't try to do it all in an afternoon. Try to copy a natural rock outcrop. The ground floor level of the rocks should slope back into the ground: half bury the back-end rocks if necessary. Pack soil between rocks; you'll need it for planting into later. Meanwhile, plant your ice plants: the best place is under your tree. Follow planting procedure as explained in other stages. Once ice plants are in, surround them with sea-washed or river-rounded pebbles. Keep your eyes and ears open for other ideas to bring a touch of the unexpected to your garden. A garden should create a sense of wonder, surprise.

75

Stage 23

Pruning is one of those essential gardening activities that too many people just shy away from. But there's no mystery to pruning: just good common sense. We illustrate the basic principles of pruning, but as you move into your second season of gardening with increased confidence, and find your skills improving with practice, you may want to check up in your library on the finer points of pruning.

Needs list: *1 can hormone rooting powder; 3 roots iceplant; 1 pkt soilless growing mix; 1 sack full of cobbles/sea-washed pebbles/similar.*
Time budget: *3 hours in 2 weeks*

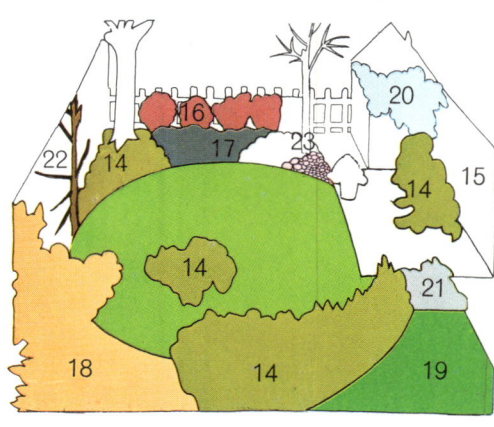

Flower of the Fortnight

The ice plant (*Sedum spectabile*) has, certainly at first glance, a rather bizarre appearance. In spite of which or perhaps because of which it's the sort of plant people rather come to love. A native of China, it grows 18 in. high, with curious blue-green leaves and stems, which are brittle and break off easily, topped by large purplish heads of flowers – made up in fact of dozens of tiny flowers. Flower colour can vary: take your pick. If you look around you'll find forms with copper coloured leaves and stems. These look most exciting grown amongst the green-leaved forms. In passing, the plant's a succulent, so you can grow it in very dry conditions, but you don't have to.

Groundwork

This is the time of year for dreaming about gardens, rather than trying to do much in them. Why not treat yourself to some gardening books, to expand on the basic knowledge you've gained from this one? If you're finding you're getting specially interested in vegetables try 'Grow Your Own Vegetables', Ward Lock Limited; if your main interest is still flowers, try 'The Flower Garden', Ward Lock Limited. If house plants fascinate you most, how about 'House Plants', Concorde Books/Ward Lock Limited? If you want your lawn to look like a bowling green, try 'The Perfect Lawn' in the same series. Ravage the shelves of bookshops for gardening books that take your fancy. Try 'Ward Lock's Complete Gardening', Ward Lock Limited, London, or 'The Rockwell's Complate Guide to Successful Gardening', Doubleday & Company. Send off for all the plant catalogues you can. Dream of gardens! Growing plants from seed needs patience. Time to cover up the Christmas rose. Put a pane of glass on sticks, or use a cloche/tent. Keeps them fresh for picking.

February weather/soil

March is the most fickle month in the gardening year. Sometimes warm, sometimes cold, never consistently either. Don't let 2 or 3 days' sun tempt you into planting early: late frosts will kill your crop. Go ahead if you can use frames, cloches, hot caps to protect the seedlings.

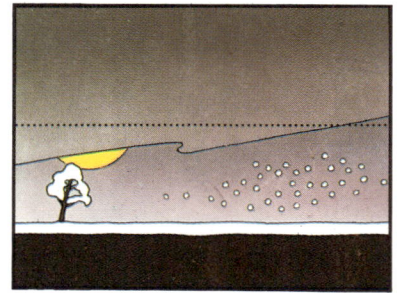

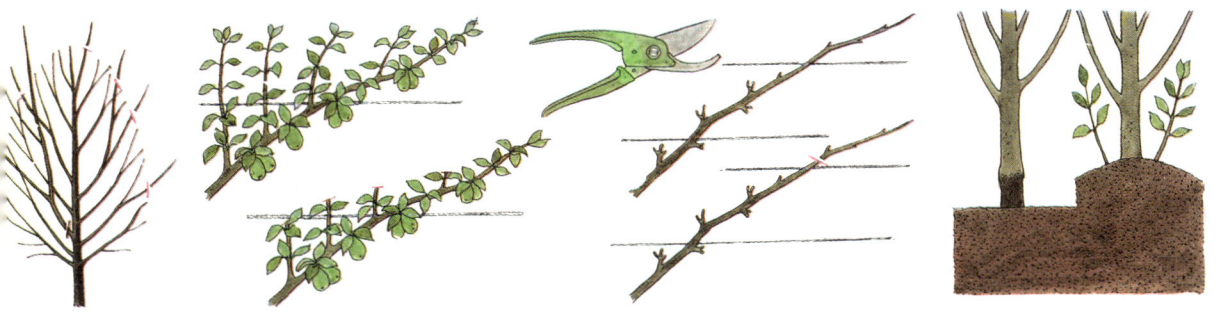

Project work: pruning: the first principles

If you've got a woody plant in your garden – shrub, tree, vine, fruit bush or tree – sooner or later you're going to want to or have to prune it. So it helps to know what pruning is all about. The purpose of pruning is to promote the growth of healthy flowering or fruiting wood by removing expendable, non-flowering or non-fruiting wood.

Basically there are only 3 ways of pruning: but you need to observe your plants to work out which to use on which. (a) Plants that flower on the current season's wood: prune out wood once flowering is over. (b) Plants that produce next year's flowers on this year's wood: prune out last year's flowering wood. (c) Slow-growing plants; just trim to shape every 2 or 3 years. Here are some specific examples. Your flowering crab: lop side-branches to keep in shape, but only do it every 2 or 3 years, and do it late summer. Pear tree: in spring, prune out dead wood. In summer, prune vertical growths of new wood back to 3 buds from the main branch. In winter cut the leading shoot back one-third of

its length. Prune any suckers away from the base anytime. Climbing rose: in sprung prune all shoots back to half their length: in summer cut out dead flower-heads and long, rampant shoots. Also prune to tidy. Vines: in autumn prune straggly growths back to firm wood close to the trellis. Cut out dead twigs and any vigorous shoots growing in directions you never asked them to grow in. Generally tidy shrubs so that they retain their natural shape. Allow them to grow together, but not so much that they crowd each other. If they do that they'll go bare at the base: looks hideous. Always take good care of your pruning tools. You don't need many. 1 good pruning knife, 1 pair pruning shears/ secateurs, 1 long-arm lopper for removing small branches from high up on trees. Rule 1 is keep all pruning tools sharp as a razor. If you can't sharpen them yourself, go back to your garden centre or return the tools to the manufacturer to sharpen for you. There's a knack to using a pruning knife: get an old hand to show you.

Stage 24

Waste not want not is a motto every good gardener should take to heart. Propagating your own plants, swapping bits with other gardeners, helps extend your garden flower-power. Plants reproduce largely by seed (sow as described in earlier stages): here we deal with non-seeding (vegetative) propagation. Take cuttings late summer: divide and layer spring or fall. Grafting's not easy: get a book from the library when you try. Buy and plant a blue Nile lily.

Needs list: *1 root agapanthus.*
Time budget: *2 hours in 2 weeks.*

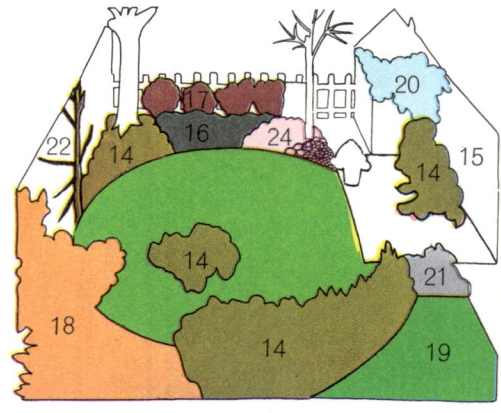

Flower of the Fortnight

Herbs are an essential part of every self-respecting garden these days. Most of them have been in cultivation for hundreds of years, and most originated in the Mediterranean basin: translated into gardening terms that means they nearly all need a sharply draining, preferably sandy soil and a position in full sun. The two we show are chives and balm. Balm is a hardy perennial, sweet-smelling and closely related to mint. Like mint, it can get out of hand. Chop it back ruthlessly if it does. The other is chives, a perennial onion with tiny bulbs, grown for its hollow, tubular leaves which have many culinary uses. Cover the herb garden with glass or clear plastic sheeting in hard winter areas.

Groundwork

Keep persevering with your compost bin. Compost does not always come right first time, but it's important that you get the hang of it. Once you've got it working it will consume most of your garden waste, and turn it into valuable top dressing and mulching material. If the compost is too wet, soggy and slow to decompose, it needs better aeration. Try a 3-in. plastic mesh netting container inside your bin, leaving a 3 in. air space between the netting and the outer framework. Alternatively, drill holes at staggered spaces in the wood container. If you really want to make the finest compost in your street, there are dozens of good, usually cheap, books on the subject. Now look at naturalizing. Weeds are plants that naturalize themselves in your garden. Get rid of the weeds and you can get many of the plants you like to naturalize there instead. Honesty and wallflowers should be starting to naturalize already: that's what all those self-sown seedlings are doing. Bulbs naturalize easily. Plant indoor hyacinths outdoors after flowering and leave them to naturalize, they'll look great.

Mid March weather/soil

The second half of March is usually rather dry – drier than April on average. However, soil-water levels are still high and the soil basically deadly chilly: bursts of warm sunshine do little to raise the soil temperature: be patient 2 more weeks.

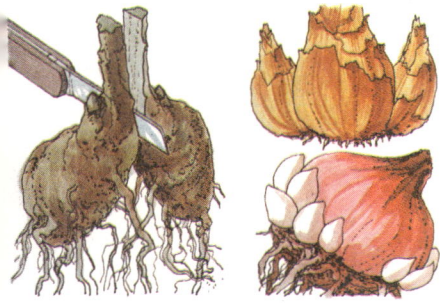

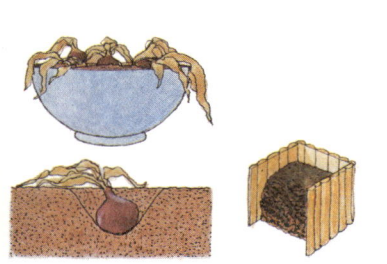

Project work: propagation and other gardening skills

Propagating your own plants is probably one of the most satisfying and creative of all aspects of gardening. There are two main types of propagation, sexual and vegetative. Sexual propagation just means sowing seeds: unless you want to go in for a plant breeding programme. You already know how to increase plants from seed, you've been doing it for nearly a year now. Time to move on to the vegetative methods: we've touched on some of them earlier. There are 4 main methods of propagating plants vegetatively: cuttings, layers, division and grafting. Let's look at each. Cuttings: two types; hardwood and softwood. Hardwood cuttings are for shrubs &c.: softwood cuttings for pelargoniums &c. Cut the piece you want to propagate with a sharp knife: make the cut just below a leaf-joint (known as a node). Strip off the lower leaves. Dip the cut end in hormone rooting powder; tap off surplus powder. (Funny stuff this hormone rooting powder: just a little helps roots develop: too much positively prevents them forming; so use it sparingly.) Plant in a V-shaped trench with sand at the bottom or in a dibbled hole in a peat pot filled with soilless growing mix. Division, at its simplest, is just splitting up root clumps, mainly of herbaceous plants. Cut dahlia tubers down to old stem with a sharp knife, leaving an 'eye' – growth bud, on each piece. Remove small bulbils from corms, bulbs. Plant up, grow on. Layering, the simplest method of all. Simply peg long shoots into the ground and cover with soil. Works for plants like periwinkle and most shrubs. Grafting is transferring the upper, fruiting or flowering part of one plant onto the rootstock of another. Read up the subject in your local library. If you want a ready checklist of how to propagate what, buy 'Handbook of Plant Propagation', Ward Lock, London, 'The Nursery Manual', Macmillan Co., New York, or 'Plant Propagation in Pictures', Doubleday & Co.

Stage 25

The gardening cycle is complete. At this stage we are back at the same time of year we started with Stage 1. We're back to the time to sow our first annual seeds for this year – this time sweet peas. We also take a look at plant diseases, fungicides, and learn a few more gardening skills. By now you should have learnt enough to be branching out on your own. There's not a heavy work-programme this fortnight so that you can put some of your own ideas into practice.

Needs list: *1 pkt sweet pea seed.*
Time budget: *1 hour in 2 weeks*

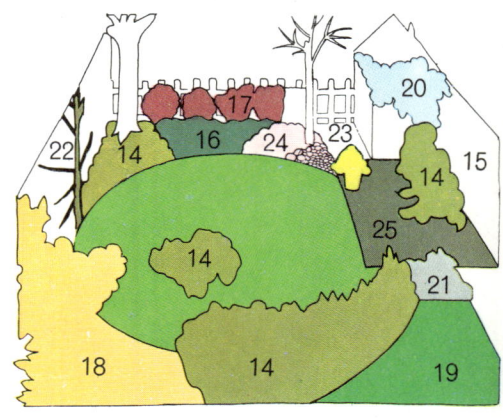

Early April weather/soil
Early April brings the weather/soil notes full cycle. This is where we came in. Air temperature is rising, and soils are warming up and drying out. Time too for you to get out into the garden and get to work again. This, your second gardening year, do project work you missed last year.

Flower of the Fortnight
Sweet peas, along with roses, chrysanthemums and dahlias, are one of the truly great garden flowers, known, grown, loved and treasured for decades. You can get sweet peas in every colour except pure yellow – and the breeders are working on that. At one time sweet peas were widely grown for the show bench: now they're usually grown just to glorify the garden. Modern dwarf strains like the Bijou sweet pea, which grows only 1 ft. high, needs only a few twigs to support it. These and the taller strains look lovely grown in circular clumps like gladioli. Prick transplants outdoors about the end of April in the bed still occupied by the spring bulbs, or any warm, sunny border.

Groundwork
Time to make a start on your lawn care programme for the year to come. Buy yourself a wire lawn rake. It's a multi-purpose tool, rakes fallen leaves, moss, old lawn clippings out of the grass, aerates it too. Rake the whole lawn, first one way, then across it at right angles to the line of the first raking. Change your mowing patterns occasionally too and mow cross-ways from time to time. Repair damaged lawn edges by cutting turves (Stage 8) replace by reversing front to back. Fill holes. Seed bare areas. Alternatively, consider supporting edges with proprietory metal or plastic edging strip. Set strip low enough in lawn to allow the mower to clear it. Later, start feeding the lawn. Keep feeding through the growing season. Prick out sweet pea seedlings (Stage 24) when they're 2 in. tall, place 10 in. apart. Put in supporting stakes, strings, wires. Care for plant gifts. Keep house plant azaleas, house plant cyclamen moist, in west window. Keep inside curtains at night. Re-pot: stand outdoors May/June. Dry off poinsettias, cut down.

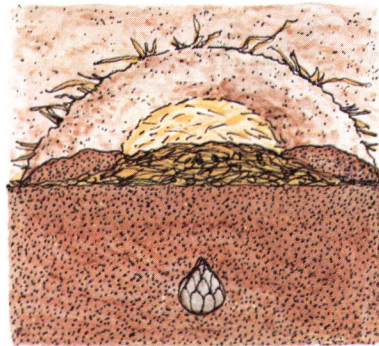

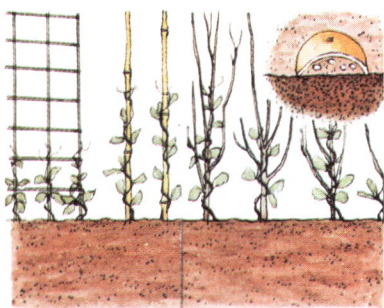

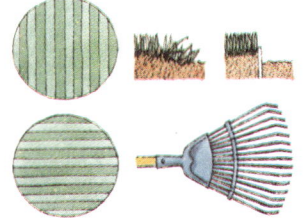

Project work: getting to know your garden

Every garden is different from every other garden. Even in a street of identical houses with gardens of identical size and shape, the differences can be substantial. It makes a difference whether the people next door or even two houses away have a fence or haven't: have a hedge or haven't. Maybe your garden is shaded by a big tree next door: or it's on the other side, casts no shade in your garden but drinks all the water from under your lawn. Get to know your garden; note the hot, dry spots; note the shaded spots which are usually cool and damp. Learn where draughts get through holes in hedges. fences, shelter belts. Grow shade-lovers in shade – sun-lovers in sun. If you live on a hillside, make a gap in the hedge/fence at the bottom of the slope to let the frost drain away (frost sinks like hot air rises). Take advantage of a sunny part of the garden to make a cold frame. Start with a second-hand window, build frame to fit. Cheats the late frosts of its last victims: gives you 2–3 weeks head start over the weather with your seeds. You can sow seed earlier, and use the frame to grow on tender young seedlings or bought-in transplants. Use cloches/tents in the same way. Protect plants against hard winter frosts by heaping bracken/straw and peat over them. Start sweet pea seeds now for summer display. Sow in soilless growing mix, in peat pots or boxes. Protect with glass (Stage 3). Use netting (Stage 3), stakes (Stage 8) or branches for supports. Protect against slugs with slug pellets. Learn a strict regime of garden hygiene: never leave diseased leaves/branches/flowers on plants. Cut off and burn them. Never leave prunings, dead vegetable matter lying around in garden. Compost bin or burn. More plants are killed, damaged, made ugly by bacteria than anything else. Hygiene helps avoid problems. Use Bordeaux mixture (ask your garden centre) against fungus diseases.

Stage 26

One first-rate climbing plant, a look back over one year in the garden, and a glimpse of the future wind up the first part of this book. If what you have learnt over the year has encouraged you to appreciate your garden, it's you who has gained by that. If you haven't had time to do everything at every stage, you've a chance to try again this year. For those full of enthusiasm, we suggest some ideas to make your garden even more rewarding in the future.

Needs list: *1 climbing hydrangea.*
Time budget: *1 hour in 2 weeks*

Mid April weather/soil

We hope by now you've learnt the intimate relationship between weather and soil conditions. Weather is unpredictable, but it does have patterns and cycles. Learn to fit your gardening activities into these patterns. As always, work with nature, not against it. Success is yours.

Flower of the Fortnight

Our final flower of the fortnight is the climbing hydrangea (*Hydrangea petiolaris*) – a plant of many virtues. It is self-clinging, trains well, will thrive even on bleak north or east walls, and is striking both in leaf and in flower. It is not rampant like many other vines – where you spend half your life tying them in and training them. It needs a little tying and trimming its first 2 or 3 years to get it to climb, but little attention after that. It is slow to start flowering, but once it does, it's a winner, turning a bare wall into something beautiful. Like so many other Japanese plants, it is highly distinctive. A deciduous plant, winter stems are one of its attractions.

Groundwork

By now the word 'chores' should have lost some of its dread for you. Garden chores aren't chores at all. They're an on-going process that not only keeps the garden tidy, but also gets things done, improves the garden, makes it easier to keep looking good week by week and year by year. Develop a routine (Stage 19): it helps you become more efficient at getting essentials done in the least time with least effort. Creates time for enjoying the garden. After all, that's what you're creating your garden for – enjoying: you're not creating it so that it simply creates more work for you for ever more. Leave space for bedding plants each year, for growing annuals, new plants and so forth. Resist the temptation to blanket the garden with shrubs. It will look dull for 10 months of the year if you do. Start reading gardening magazines, getting together gardening books. Complete schedule of chores by planting climbing hydrangea at foot of chosen wall. Move bulbs to shaded corner to let the leaves die off naturally: replace with bedding plants.

Project work: more plants, more ideas

So far we've only made a start on the area behind the house. By now you should know enough to invent your own design for the area in front of your house. Apply the principles we applied to your back yard; adapt the back yard design to fit the front. Like simply take a half or a quarter of the back yard design and use that as the design for your front area. Ring a few changes. Swap some things left to right. Use different shrubs, and a different tree. Some suggestions: try a mountain ash/rowan = *Sorbus aucuparia*, good bark, medium flowers, good leaves, brilliant fruits. Try weeping standard roses. And why not a hanging basket over the porch (get your garden centre to show you how to plant it) – perhaps a window box. Start from the same basic ideas, but make it new, make it different. Follow the same work schedule for the front as you did for the back, and success will be yours. A few more ambitious ideas for your back garden. How about a greenhouse? Lots of fun: money-saving too in the long run, since you can grow masses of seedlings there very cheaply. Invest in a garden shed: best place to keep tools, mower &c. Build yourself a vine-covered pergola for the patio. Follow the same basic construction principles as for erecting the trellis. Place a fountain near the rockery amid the brightly painted stones under the flowering crab. Great fun, and the sound of trickling water always brings a garden to life. Then treat yourself to some garden furniture for the patio.

12 Months in

After 12 months and a mere 104 hours work, does your garden look anything at all like the artist's impression shown here of how our baseplan garden should look by now?

O.K. so you may feel just a little disappointed because there may be less colour in the garden now than there was at the 6 month mark, but there's a good reason for that. That was high summer, the most floriferous time of year. It's a fairly dead time of year now: a moment of waiting; everything in your garden should be bursting at the buds and just about to bring you the most colourful, trouble-free year you've ever had in your garden.

If you took colour shots of your garden before you started our work programme, get them out and gloat over them. They give you a true comparison from which you can chart your real progress, because those snaps of 12 months ago were taken at the same time of year. Even if you haven't achieved all you hoped for, the differences should be enormous. Changing the shape of the lawn should have made the garden relax, and invite you to go out into it. Other permanent features like the patio, the ground cover plants, the ornaments all help to turn a dump into a garden. Shrubs, trees, climbers and herbaceous plants will all burst into growth soon, and each year they will give a better and better display, and you'll have less work to do. Then there are hidden assets: like the way you have revitalized your soil. Now you've got your compost bin working smoothly, keep on mulching the soil, to suppress weeds and feed the plants.

You've got a year's gardening experience behind you. The confidence of your achievements, the knowledge you've gained from your mistakes, plus a refreshing and novel way of looking at gardens that means you can move on to greater things if you want. Like adapting ideas from the gardens illustrated and described in Part 11 of this book to a particular corner of your own garden. And you've got the know-how and experience to do it yourself.

Meanwhile, it's time to report again on the progress made by our 6 volunteer gardeners. You can see how they fared on the following pages.

Recap of workplans 14-26

Colour key code recap
1 = Bean bed
2 = Annuals bed
3 = Covering vines
4 = Summer display bed
5 = Autumn display bed
6 = Patio
7 = Container plants
8 = Lawn
9 = Summer bedding plants
10 = Vegetable patch
11 = Cottage garden/perennial corner
12 = Compost bin
13 = Ornamental tree
14 = Bulb bed
15 = Trellis
16 = Permanent ground cover
17 = Living hedge
18 = Shrub bed
19 = Herbaceous border
20 = Climbing roses
21 = Herb bed
22 = Fan-trained tree
23 = Decoration
24 = Rockery/rock garden
25 = Patio paving
26 = Christmas present plants

This page, like page 54, is simply a resume of pages 14/15 and 18/19 – an instant guide to the colours and numbers that relate to the workplans for the whole 26 stages of your garden-making activities. Use it to check up on your own progress, and on the progress of the 6 volunteer gardeners – as well as a quick guide to what the colours and numbers all mean on the plans we adapted from our basic groundplan to fit the different needs of the different gardens and gardeners.

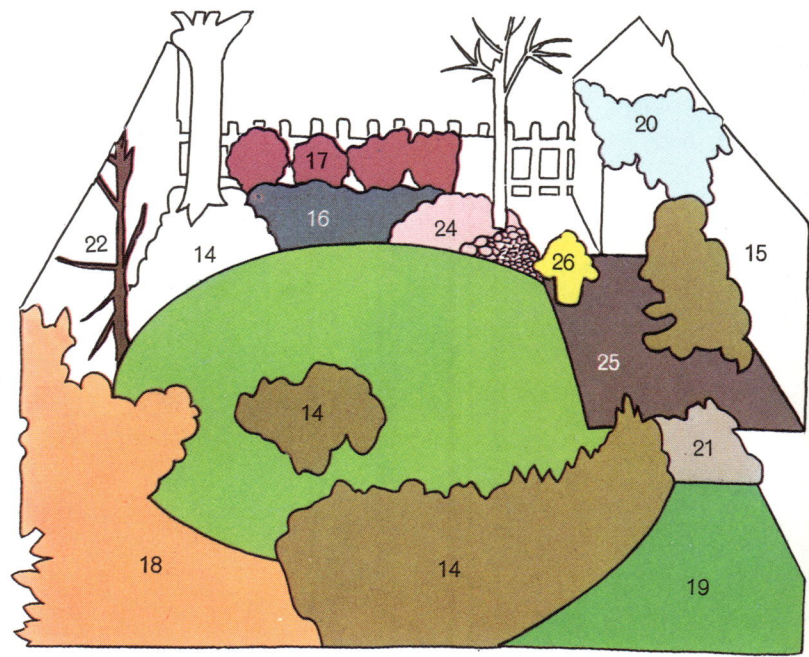

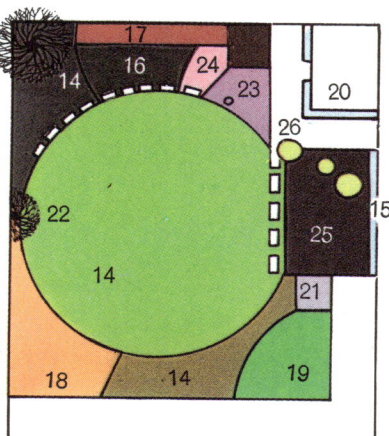

Where work projects in the second half of the gardening year are sited in areas that were planted during the earlier growing season, identical or similar colours are used for both periods. Thus bulbs are the same colour as the annuals were, and so on.

The Trial Gardens

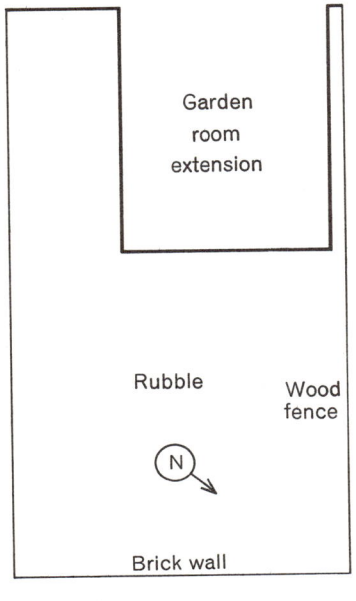
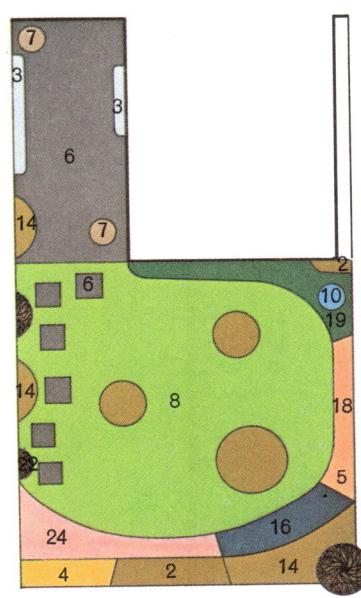

Out of the chaos of their builders' tip they started with Michael and Angela Harding created a varied and casual town garden. Angela wanted the garden to be visually appealing rather than productive. She decided not to attempt any of the more functional features – such as a compost heap – or vegetables. Carrots and celery are excepted. Next season they plan to fill some of the patio pots with miniature tomato plants. Apart from nasturtiums and sunflowers, they will not repeat the annuals. Herbaceous plants – lupins, Canterbury bells, hollyhocks and foxgloves – will give summer colour. The brightest winter splash appeared unexpectedly: a rhododendron, gleaned from a nearby demolition site, burst into flower one week after planting.

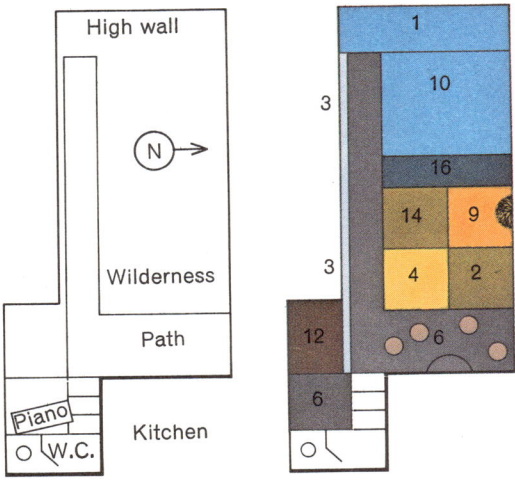

William James did not touch his garden after the summer, and 12 months after he started it looked rather worse than when he began. The scrub grass became a mud patch, the birds he wanted to encourage no longer visit. Deeply despondent about the poor showing of annuals, his apathy set in around August. Although he says he is not a born gardener, we feel that if he had followed the action plans right through, he would have built a foundation of sturdy shrubs and perennials, well able to survive the dark conditions of his walled-in, prison-like garden. We feel too, that several weeks spent cycling across the Andes broke the work-plan so radically that his best bet would have been to leave it and start again next spring. But now he has decided to sit back – and await the return of the wilderness.

87

With the smallest of the test gardens, Kenneth and Heather MacLeod were restricted not only by lack of space but by the fact that they already had most of the basic features of the *Two-Hour Garden* So we were not too disppointed to see the comments on Mrs MacLeod's fortnightly reports – no trellis work done – already erected; no room in garden for further cover plants; no hedge planted – no room; and so on. We were pleased that she was able to apply so many of our decorative ideas. Last March there was nothing further from their minds than a vegetable patch, yet the runner beans were so successful that they plan more next year – and possibly some soya beans as well. They will add parsley, fennel, chives, tarragon and garlic to the herb garden. Mrs MacLeod reports a distinct soil improvement – but 'the most striking feature has been the colour'.

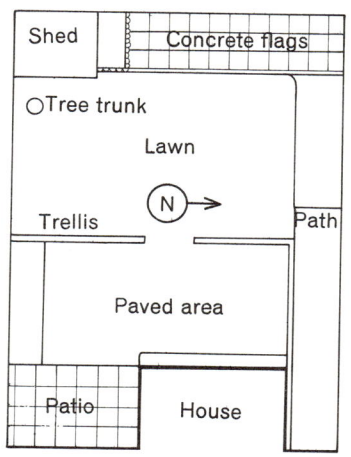
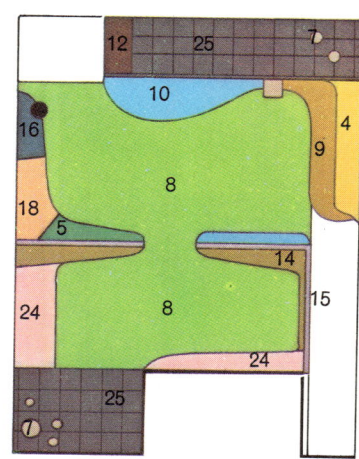

With a garden twice as large as any of the others, we expected the Allans to exceed vastly our needs list and time budget. But surprisingly this has not been so, though they did buy seven bushes for their hedges instead of two, and bought twice our recommended number of bulbs. The ideas he found particularly useful were moisture conservation (Stage 7), our advice on indoor plants (Stage 21) – and our continuous emphasis on soil improvement. He feels that this year he has gained the experience essential for carrying on with confidence, and – as he has laid the crazy paving – with as little extra work as possible.

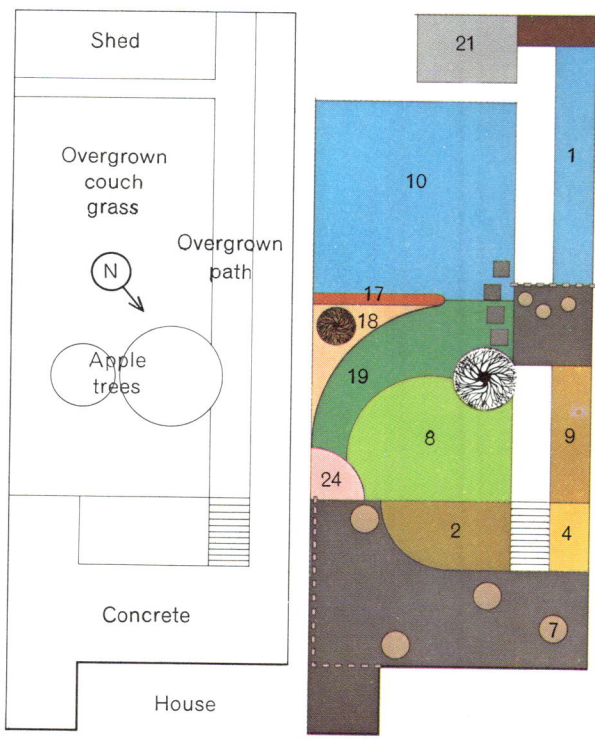

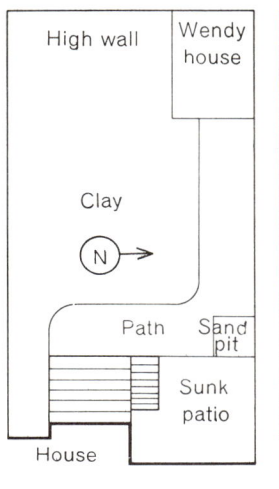
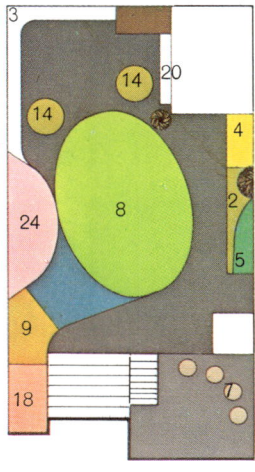

Timothy and Penelope Hicks achieved much more variety in their garden than is usual for this time of year. Each border was dark with peat, the patio had been newly painted, and the tulips had flowered weeks early. The Hickses were delighted. With a few imaginative additions – a marble wall seat, a green plant-filled bottle – they kept closely to each stage. 'There's no doubt about it, we would never have done it without the discipline of the plan. If you read a gardening book you have to read the whole book – *then* do it step-by-step. We got a terrific amount of pleasure with not much effort. And we learnt. We did not have a great success with the annuals, but we learnt that we did not want big things, we want squat things – that is why we particularly went for dwarf tulips.

Michael Thorpe was furious when we visited him. 'Everything is late. The nursery sent the shrubs late, the lawn arrived only three weeks ago. It's in an awful condition, caked with mud.' Their garden presented problems. Last spring it took weeks to clear the rubble. Yet we feel that the Thorpes' is potentially the most interesting of all the test gardens. A first task next year is to build a right-hand wall; then they have more ambitious ideas: to make the rafters overhanging the kitchen window serve as the roof of a greenhouse and the floor of a flower-hung balcony; and to build curving wood steps from the balcony to the perennial border below. In order to plan for exciting colour contrast in the shrubbery, Michael has drafted a month-by-month scale diagram showing exactly what will be in bloom when.

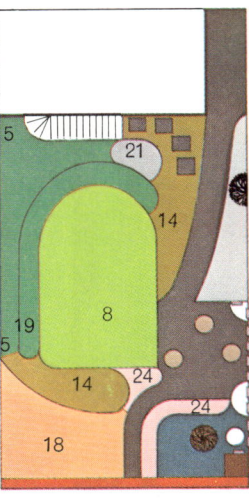

Part Two

The Gardens

Branching Out on Your Own

You may not know all there is to know about gardening – you probably never will and if you ever did you'd die of boredom – but after the 26 stages you've worked your way through spread over 52 weeks and 104 hours work, you have at least acquired all the basic skills of gardening. And if this book has opened your mind to new horizons, shown you that gardening can be fun, that finding out about gardening can be an adventure, if you've found that chores aren't bores and that a small amount of knowledge is a tremendous stimulus to finding out even more, then all the work that has gone into the making of this book has been worthwhile. Because now you're on your own.

In the first part of this book we took you step by step through the various stages of designing a garden, and bringing that design into being. This part is rather different. All we do here is throw out a lot of highly stimulating ideas. It's entirely up to you to turn them into realities if you want to. There are just ideas: no plans, no stages, no project work. It's up to you to work those out for yourself. You have the basic skills; you should have the confidence. You've done more difficult things already than many of the ideas thrown out here. Probably the only thing you won't have is the space to carry out all the ideas you want to. Which is a blessing in disguise.

Because if you tried to have a little corner of every one of the gardens that follow in this section, your garden would be a mess. It would have no sense of design, no cohesion, no harmony. Happily human nature and space limitations plus a pinch of your own good sense will probably save you from that disaster. You may have never had a chance to discover this for yourself before – and a garden gives you a better chance to do it than most people realize – but every human being has a very strong, fundamental drive towards creativity. What you express when you create something is your own personality. You express that personality when you furnish your home: similarly you express it when you create your garden. Because you're a unique human being, some ideas will interest you, others won't. Different ideas would interest someone else. That fact limits which of the gardens that follow will appeal to you. Without much conscious effort on your part, the ideas you choose to put into execution in your garden will all have one common link – the mere fact that they interested you. That in itself will make them cohere – provided you stick to one fundamental principle.

A garden must have unity. If you've faithfully followed the stages so far, you will have a garden that has unity, a garden that is drawn together around that circular central lawn. The simplest way of taking ideas from the gardens that follow and making them your own, is to incorporate them into the areas surrounding that unifying central lawn. You could, for example, have a pleached or espaliered walk down the path by the patio, a damp and shady garden under the large old tree, and a hanging garden on a boundary wall.

The other simple alternative is to make your whole garden over to one of the garden ideas that you'll come to in a minute. Some ideas, like the secret garden, just don't fit readily into the urban or suburban garden, unless you give the whole thing over to them. In large gardens, of course, things are simpler. You simply make the garden into a series of interconnecting compartments, and each compartment can be as different as you like from the one before.

Before you branch out on your own, try to define for yourself what you think your garden ought to be or do. Is it a place to be busy gardening in? Is it a place in which to relax? Is it for the kids or for you or for both? Is it there, like a picture, to be looked at, or is it more like an extension of the house, part of the home, an extra room, to be lived in? It's probably a bit of all those things, but mostly it's the last, a place to be lived in. So plan your garden round the way you live.

Lastly, remember that while a garden should be visually exciting, it should also be restful. Try to strike a happy medium between vibrantly garish colours and the quieter effects of contrasts of foliage, both colour-wise and size and texture-wise. Mix gold and grey and bronze foliage among the greens, and large bold leaves among smaller ones or finely divided ones. And try to strike a happy medium between giving yourself so much work in the garden that you never have time to do anything else, and having just enough to do in the garden to keep your interest and curiosity alive. Always have at least one more new plan to put into execution the next year and the next year and the next.

The Ornamental Garden

Ornaments evoke a world of fantasy, so it is not surprising they have been used as embellishments from the earliest gardens. Some have a use, such as furniture, others are there to excite the imagination and create moods. In some great country garden that has seen better days, one will sometimes come across the half-buried bust of a Greek goddess peering out from under an overgrown rhododendron bush, creating an atmosphere far more emotive than when the statue was still on its pedestal, set on a

terrace. In fact, the secret of using an ornament in your garden often lies in artful concealment from the immediate view, so that it is revealed unexpectedly as you move around. The biggest single item of ornament is the plant container; most gardens have one of one kind or another. Small ornaments are cheaper to buy but much harder to position than, say, a large block of carved stonework from a demolished building. Keep your eyes open for whatever appeals to you.

The Miniature Garden

Unusually small plants with fine stems and leaves are grown in miniature gardens. People whose gardens are restricted to a balcony or patio can make good use of them, finding that though the space is 'mini', the plants themselves do not have to be miniature: astute judgment is needed in the choice of plants for this kind of garden. Diminutive plants are wasted at ground level, unless they are used like a green carpet as described in Stage 16. Rockeries bring plants closer to the eye, so do containers on pedestals, window sills, ledges and so forth; in these, the delicate beauty of alpines and small plants is fully revealed. A simple version of the miniature garden is a **cacti bowl**, decorated with coloured pebbles, larger stones and pieces of mirror. **Terracotta strawberry pots**, ringed with planting cups, are particularly suitable for moving outdoors on to the terrace in summer. Varieties of succulent plants, such as sempervivums and sedums, make a bizarre but convincing miniature hanging garden. **Indoor bottle gardens** are popular too, not difficult. The **sink or trough** is the favourite way to make a miniature garden, providing space for elaborate garden layouts; rocks, pools, stepping stones, bridges, pergolas, temples and other ornaments can be arranged in it, in just a few square feet of space. Remember the following three points for this kind of miniature garden.

Location: find the proper place in your main garden, avoiding extremes of heat, damp, shade, exposure, drip from trees, and find the most sheltered spot.

Setting: most difficult to determine, for if the miniature garden is too close to other plants the effect is spoiled, and if it is too prominent, it can look a little ridiculous. Miniature garden troughs look well, set in the herb garden, as many herbs have fine leaves and subdued colouring. A neutral background such as a sheltering wall or fence is also effective.

Soil and drainage: a third of the depth should be a drainage layer, and peat should cover this to stop the compost from washing away. Use a soil-based growing mixture, your own fine, well-drained and fibrous mix. There is an enormous range of alpine plants available for the miniature garden, some of which are grown as 'lawns'. Among the shrubs – dwarf roses come in several varieties, and dwarf deciduous and coniferous trees range from the prostrate and the bushy to the thin cylindrical needle. These plants are available as seeds, but it means waiting longer for your complete garden.

The Paved Garden

The traditions of China and Japan have given a new dimension to western garden design. To make a paved garden with some of the feeling of the East, it is not necessary to study the intricate principles of the Japanese garden. The garden in our illustration is based on a completely paved area (foreground) merging into areas where paving and low planting are about equal. The fully paved terrace takes the hard wear; it is paved with cement tiles, but natural materials are more sympathetic to the garden. Stone fragments can be used for crazy paving; stones and tiles set in prostrate ground-cover plants lead from the centre of this garden to areas of pebbles, gravel, sand and discs of wood from tree trunks sawn across. Choice of plants depends on the wear expected: fine fescue grasses and chamomile are toughest; next come thyme varieties, the sagina varieties (Pearlwort), sedum varieties; lastly moss. The relative amount of sun and shade influences plant choice. Still water is most effective in a paved garden as it helps to bring the plane of the earth closer to the sky. Behind the pool, members of the pink, saxifrage, campanula, veronica, heather and other alpine plant families form dense mats – like a paving of green. Patterns of curving shapes are formed by beds of small, rounded boulders, gravel and raked sand; rocks appear singly or in groups. Against such a background of surface textures, individual trees are striking – especially when they have unusual trunks, branches, leaves. In the background a 'forest' of dwarf coniferous trees in a wide range of foliage colours reflects the statuesque form of the boulders. The paved garden must be tidied and kept neat much in the way a hedge is pruned. Where large stone pieces are needed for areas among dwarf trees, artificial 'hollow stone' can be bought, and most gardens will need extra peaty soil as this is the most satisfactory medium for many rock plants. The eye soon becomes accustomed to the miniature landscape and notices details which are quite lost in an ordinary garden, but because detail is so important a high standard of maintenance is required. Something as little as a footprint on the raked sand can mar it all.

The Town and

If all the open space you have is a roof, a modest balcony, or just a window-box or front-door steps, there are many things you can do to bring to it a breath of the countryside.

Lay some Astroturf (simulated grass) and combine it with loose white gravel chippings to form 'paths' (as in our picture). Next door's chimney stack could be forgotten behind a painted trellis covered in creeper.

Barrel-tubs are invaluable: you could content yourself with variegated ivy, but the ambitious could try a small ornamental tree such as a flowering dogwood, or a Dracaena. The square tub could be planted with wandering clematis or rhododendron, and the neat pergola effect round the window is created by the combination of clematis and birdcage.

A storage area is useful if space permits, perhaps hidden under a tray of summer pot plants – tuberous begonias or zonal-leafed geraniums.

In order to keep weight down, a low retaining wall can be made. With soil-less compost instead of earth, it makes an excellent bed for scented-leafed geraniums and French marigolds. Finally, try a moss-lined hanging basket planted

Roof Garden

with weeping lobelia, petunias and fuschias.

Below the garden our artist has illustrated two window boxes, one filled with herbs, the other with sweet William and Shirley poppy. Give old window boxes a new look with ceramic tiles.

If you really want to go to town on your roof garden, want to import tons of earth, add a swimming pool, a rockery, huge specimen trees, there's just one very but very important thing you must check up on. Quite simply whether your roof is or is not strong enough to carry the weight of all these things. There's no simple way you can work this out for yourself. You'll have to call in a structural engineer, get the whole structure checked out for the weight it can carry. It's probably worth doing this even with a relatively unambitious plan. It is quite surprising how light soilless growing mixes are when you lug them up to the roof when they are dry, and how incredibly heavy they are when they are planted up and wet. It's all too easy to underestimate the weightload. And it just is not fun to find the petunias and Shirley poppies, together with the half-dead goldfish landing on your bed in the middle of the night.

The Historical Garden

There is a growing interest in historical gardens, particularly those of the late Middle Ages and Tudor times. There are fine examples to be seen; a Tudor garden at Kew and a great colonial American garden at Williamsburg, Virginia. A principal feature was their seclusion, walled and enclosed. They give us the feeling of entering another, more peaceful world. Starting at the top left of our garden is an arbour shaped as a long tunnel formed by trees planted very closely together in a double row. A metal or wooden frame is used to train the trees to form a dense canopy, their branches are intertwined and pruned. Seats line the tunnel, which makes a cool, refreshing place to relax in in hot weather. Apple, hornbeam, laburnum, wisteria and grape vines are effective. Behind the arbour is the mount, a symbolic feature of ancient origin in garden design: a narrow, diagonal path – bordered by box plants – circles to a sundial at the summit; long, low, stone flower boxes, which act as seats, are filled with carpet plants such as thyme – giving off delightful fragrances when crushed. Shade is provided by a mulberry tree. To the right is the orchard. Many trees are trained as espaliers against the wall; the less hardy fruits are most suited to this form of cultivation and look most decorative. The knot garden or *parterre* runs down to the right from the orchard, its miniature hedges of rosemary forming geometrical panels in which such flowers as sweet William, carnations, heliotrope and pansy are grown. The trellis is smothered with old varieties of rose noted for their fragrance and delicate colours: damasks, bourbons, gallicas, moss and cabbage roses. The fountain is designed to accentuate the sound of falling water. In the foreground is part of the herb garden, entered by an archway on the right, which, like the wall, is covered with vines such as ivy, honeysuckle and summer jasmine. Herbs are grown in panels according to their various uses. Against the wall are hollyhock, crown imperial lily, Jerusalem cross (Lychnis), columbine and double daisies – among the oldest garden flowers. An historical garden requires a pattern of simple, straight paths and small spaces leading from one to another, so that you cannot see everything in the garden at once. A delightful sense of mystery and surprise is created by this unfolding of gardens within a garden. Indeed, some of the greatest of the modern gardens of this century have been created on the gardens within gardens principle.

The Secret Garden

Generations of children and grown-ups have been enchanted by *The Secret Garden* of Frances Hodgson Burnett. A door in a wall ... a private world where flowers and trees and wild creatures are quietly getting on with their own lives. A beautiful idyll, it is one many can share by creating the essence in secret corners of their gardens. Some suggestions. Build a wooded rock garden – small trees clipped into formal topiary shapes, growing close together out of a rock-strewn earth; they merge into a common silhouette. Brightly coloured flowers carpet the rocks, emphasising the straight, trunks of the trees. If you are the happy possessor or would-be creator of a secret walled garden, you will have enclosing walls smothered in vines and ivy, where time, sunlight and nature are held between four walls. The way in is a door in one of those walls. A secret garden walled in with hedges is an easier proposition. A big variety of hedge plants is available, from the evergreen, slow-growing hollies and yews, to the fast-growing Leyland's cypress. Among deciduous hedges, beech and hornbeam are unequalled. A maze represents the height of hedge cultivation, and perhaps the most secret of secret gardens. A large-scale maze demands great space for layout. Within the scope of average gardens you can form a maze for the summer: sow lines of maize; or string a maze pattern of annual vines on trellises. A small retreat can be made with a free-standing curved hedge. Our illustration shows three curving hedges which form two narrow passageway entrances at one end, and a wide opening at the other; the ground is hollowed, allowing for a natural pool with water plants; the grass is allowed to grow quite long so that plants in the lawn can flower. The tree-house is an effective way of retreating from the world. If you have an old tree that has died back to the trunk, saw off the branches to the point where they can still support a platform. Plant a couple of Russian vines or *Rosa filipes* 'Kiftsgate' at the base, and within two years you will have a 'lollipop house' which can be trimmed or left woolly. Make a jungle-like approach to it with hedges trimmed to fantastic shapes.

The Hanging Garden

This garden of creeping, weeping and hanging plants should appeal to the lazy streak in us all. Maintenance is reduced because weeds have to compete with plants that are equally aggressive. It is surprising, too, how many people fail to exploit the wall to wall carpeting character of familiar vines, which will grow well horizontally or festoon downwards over walls. Virginia creepers (*Parthenocissus* species) are particularly adept, but so are clematis (*Clematis montana* 1), and honeysuckle (*Lonicera* species). Russian vine (*Polygonum baldschuanicum* 2) will do anything, and quickly. Cover sheds, smother trees, tumble over walls, a billowing green mass, white with flower panicles in late summer. It just scrambles up wherever it goes. Winter jasmine (*Jasminum nudiflorum* 3), if not trained, flops about in a chaotic but attractive fashion. The formidably named *Lamium galeobdolon variegatum* 4) almost equals the Russian vine: a spreading perennial, the long, trailing stems root as they go. It has marbled silver leaves and is excellent in shady, dampish places. *Lamium maculatum* 5), mentioned in Stage 6, is a neater spreader. Nearly every shrub family has at least one member which creeps, weeps or hangs: *Rosa paulii* 6) makes a dense, low thicket, smothering everything, and flowering profusely. *Cotoneaster horizontalis* 7) and *Cotoneaster dammeri* 8) grow in wide-spreading carpets, the former to some extent up walls, the latter trailing over every obstacle. *Viburnum tomentosum* 9) is pancake-shaped, with long, quite horizontal branches. Rose of Sharon (*Hypericum calycinum* 10) will thrive in most difficult conditions; it is as tenacious as a weed. Many spreading herbaceous plants have colourful flowers; the bellflower family (*Campanula carpatica* 11), and the geraniums (*Geranium endressii* 12) are examples. For year-round colour, the evergreen ivy family (Hedera 13 and 14) is outstanding with many varieties all neat, low-growing on the ground, and uniform just like a lawn. Similarly, the ground-hugging conifers (*Juniperus horizontalis glauca* 15) provide variety, especially in the gold and silver variegated kinds. Heathers (*Calluna* and *Erica* varieties 16) are a unique family of creeping plants providing a garden of their own. Once established, easy to manage, they flower most months of the year.

Carex pendula
(sedge)
Iris kaempferi
(herbaceous plant)
Deschampia
cespitosa
(grass)
Lawn
Paving slabs
Verticle
pipe
Drainage
layer
Weep
holes
Very shallow gradient
Perforated plastic irrigation pipes
Impermeable
membrane

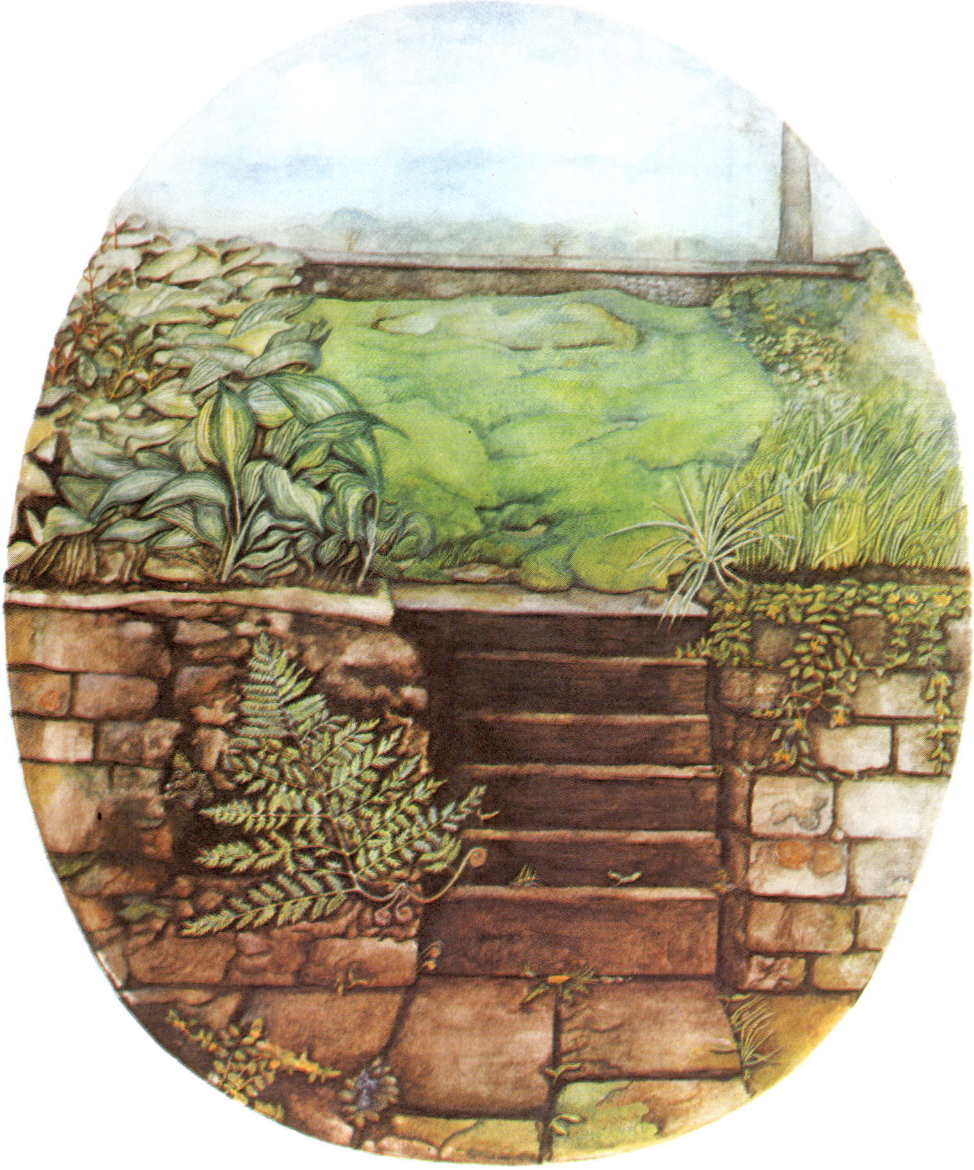

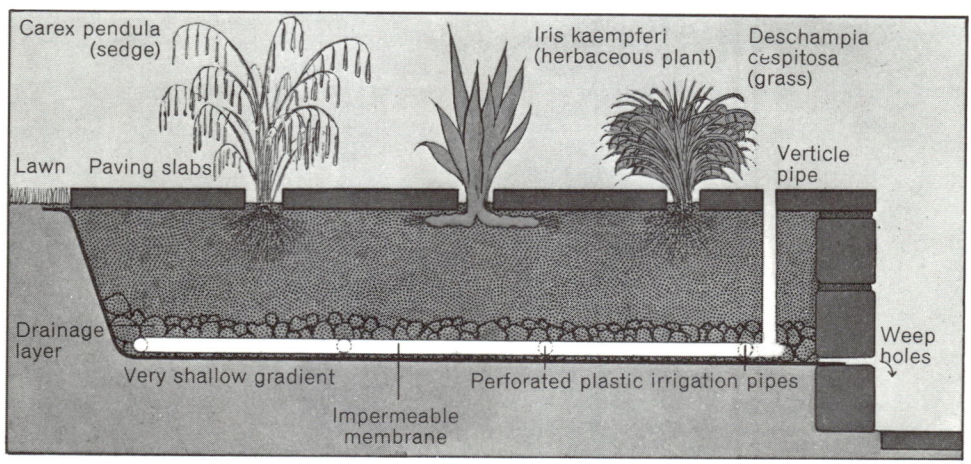

The Damp and Shady Garden

The Victorians learnt how to make a virtue out of damp and shady places in the garden, so the revival of interest in popular plants of this period has included varieties suitable for such conditions. Many have flowers of delicate or unusual colouring such as the green hellebores, or leaves which are excellent for flower arrangements in the house.

Our illustration shows a flight of steps leading up from a flagstoned basement path into a shady part of the garden. Self-sown mosses and grasses are in the joints of the path, and a fern grows in the crevice of the wall. Lichens are a sign of pure air, as they do not tolerate atmospheric pollution.

Nurseries offer an exciting range of hardy ferns besides those which occur naturally. Most are ideal for damp shade.

The wild perennial ground covers shown are the yellow-flowered creeping Jenny (*Lysimachia nummularia*) and the bronze and blue spikes of bugle (*Ajuga reptans*). Introduce the variegated dead nettle *Lamium maculatum*, or its varieties '*Album*' and '*Aureun*', and – provided there is not too much traffic on the path – the dense, carpeting rosettes of London pride (*Saxifraga umbrosa*).

Variegated *Hosta crispula* at the top of the wall represents the 20 odd varieties of this family, outstanding for plants that thrive in cool, shady places. The Christmas rose or hellebores contrast well with the hosta, having deeply divided leaves.

In places where lawns will not grow properly, let grasses and sedges mature into their flowering and fruiting stages – they have a beauty of their own. Here *Carex morrowii*, a sedge, and *Holcus mollis* 'Variegatus', are planted at the top of the wall. The best known variegated grass is gardener's garters (*Phalaris arundinacea* 'Picta'), but it spreads unduly if not checked.

Dig soil to 18 in., and lay perforated plastic pipes on a heavy-quality plastic sheet. Leave vertical pipes at intervals, in order to feed the subterranean irrigation system in very dry weather. Collect rainwater from roofs in water butts/barrels for watering (never make a damp bed if you have to rely all the time on tap water). Backfill first 3 in. with crocks, etc., then a peat-soil mix. *Drainage* and *aeration* are essential, so see that excess water can seep away through 'weep' holes in any retaining wall. Laying paving on the damp bed cuts down water evaporation and gives plants a cool root-run.

The Invalid Garden

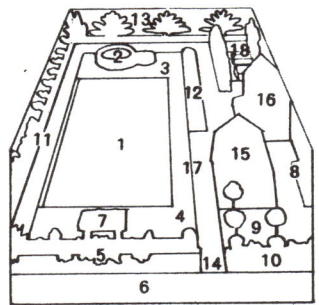

Gardening is therapy. Its therapeutic value is all the greater for the elderly, the disabled and especially those in wheelchairs. With the help of carefully planned gardens and specially designed tools, gardening can bring them immense pleasure.

First and foremost, the layout must meet the handicapped gardener's requirements. The priorities are safety and convenience. There is a good-sized lawn (1), uncluttered by beds and therefore easier to mow, with a raised pond (2) – safer than a sunken one – built on concrete openwork (3) which is suitable for a wheelchair. This openwork is extended to the near end of the garden (4), providing an alternative path near a terraced flower bed (5) dividing patio (6) from lawn. This raised bed and the raised trough garden (7), the alpine shelf (8), the bay trees in tubs (9) and a wall garden for growing herbs (10) are all within easy reach of a wheelchair and at comfortable working height (about 2 ft. high); the borders, which are at ground level (11 and 12), are kept narrow to save the back from bending and stretching, and the border which edges the lawn (12) is filled with plants that do not need staking. Also easily within reach from the path are the fan peach and apricot trees (13). The path is most important; this one is non-slip and reaches every corner of the garden. A ramp (14) leads from the smooth, even tiles of the patio to garden level. The greenhouse (15) and potting shed (16) stand near each other beside the path. Watering: to avoid the danger of tripping over hoses left lying around, a water pipe (17) is laid beside the path, sockets are placed around the garden into which short lengths of hose are inserted for watering. The compost heap (18) is well out of the way, but still accessible; it cannot sprawl unmanageably as it is kept in wire mesh. The main thing to bear in mind when planning a garden for anyone confined to a wheel chair or otherwise disabled, is that invalids are far less able to cope with knocks and falls than the rest of us. The garden must be planned to avoid these dangers. All work areas must be easily accessible.

A wheelchair gardener tending a raised bed about 2 ft. high

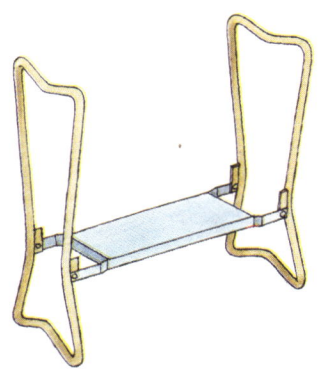

The Easi-kneeler has strong supports; serves as a stool

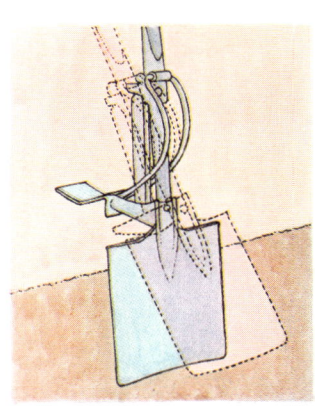

The Wolf Terrex spade has a foot pedal: for easy digging

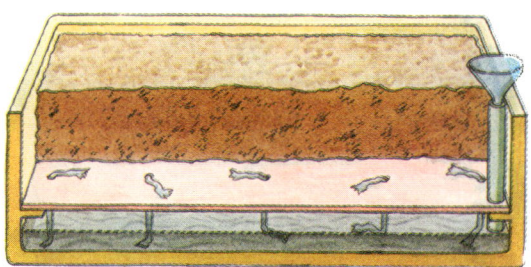

B Container with automatic irrigation for several plants

C Section of terrarium showing mains lead and light fitting

Terrarium which includes flowering African violets and flowering orchids, with overhead lighting

The Indoor Garden

Indoors is a peculiar situation for plants, because the 'climate' of homes is not really like that of a natural habitat, even for a shade-loving species. Moisture/humidity, temperature and light are crucial factors. Moisture meters are available for accurate measurement of soil conditions, but humidity is something you provide and test yourself. Put the plant pot into a larger container and fill the space with damp peat (never allow to dry out) to give local humidity (A). The peat acts as a damp blanket for the soil in the pot and soaks up excessive water. Artificial light makes many areas in the home available for plants which otherwise would be unsuitable. Fluorescent light tubes must be used. The strength of the light should be equivalent to a light-meter reading in dull weather, the fixture placed about 1 ft. away from foliage. A light fixture can be combined with a more sophisticated container for several plants, in which automatic irrigation is used (B). The terrarium is the ultimate refinement (C). Its unique advantage is complete climate control, a kind of plant aquarium – the bottle garden is a primitive version. Any space can have a terrarium fitted into it; alternatively, they can be left mobile to be plugged in wherever needed. The glass case has a non-corrodible metal or wooden frame, sliding doors, and electrical fittings to control the heating and the lighting units. A thermostat inside the case controls the temperature. The plant container no longer needs a reservoir as the terrarium has a relatively small moisture loss to the outside, but for plants requiring a 'sticky' atmosphere a reservoir could be incorporated into the case. The versatility of the method is only limited by plant size, but it is particularly suitable for the cultivation of indoor flowering plants. *Warning*: considerable care is needed in the electrical installation and testing of these units; all work must be expertly carried out and readily accessible. There has never been a bigger choice of house plants: start with the easy ones – some suppliers identify the relative easiness of their plants – and as skill in cultivation is acquired, move on to the more unusual. In planting a bottle garden or terrium several options are open to you. You can landscape them, using small rocks, polished pebbles, sea-washed drift-wood: or you can create small streams through them, especially suitable for terraria, in which you can grow miniature tropical water plants. Hygiene is important in all enclosed plantings. Always remove fallen leaves and flowers.

The Conservatory Garden

A conservatory differs from a greenhouse in being a part or an extension of your home. It offers scope for the imagination. You can take your cue perhaps from the colonial atmosphere captured in a Somerset Maugham play: cool sweeping palms, hanging baskets, mirrors, Nile green washed walls and rush matting; or the cloistered stillness of the traditional English conservatory, with flagstone floors, hanging vines and walls softened with panels of stained, etched or smoked glass. **Choosing conservatory plants**: Many growers now grade their plants into easy, intermediate or delicate. For example: *Hedera* Heisse (Heisse's ivy) (1), *Asplenium nidus-avis* (bird's nest fern) (2), *Rhoicissus rhomboidea* (grape ivy) (3), and *Cissus antarctica* (kangaroo vine) (4), all easy to grow; peperomias (5 and 6), *Ficus benjamina* (weeping fig) (7), and various palms (8), all intermediate; *Fittonia verschaffeltii* (snakeskin plant) (9) and *Croton* hybrid (Joseph's coat) (10), delicate. Add geraniums (11), a grape vine (12), bulbs and perhaps a containerised tree and you have a good start. **Constructing the conservatory**: if converting a room into a conservatory, including one in the design of a house, or purchasing an extension unit in kit form or specially made, here are some important points. *Flooring*: make the floor easy to swab down or brush up – wooden planks, flagstones, quarry tiles or plain concrete. *Staging*: should be solid with a skimming of gravel, or slatted easy access height. *Watering*: make sure a tap or tank are installed. Also available: small perforated pipe lines that lie in the soil, and automatically release water when the earth gets too dry. *Heating*: consult heating engineers; install a thermostat. A fountain (15) and an aviary (16) make pretty additions to the Conservatory Garden; there are many other imaginative ideas for this garden in a house, which ensures year-round gardening without necessarily having to go out of doors.

The Bulb Garden

January, Crocus ancyrensis

February, Iris danfordiae

March, Ipheion

Crocus species flower from autumn to spring, many naturalize freely. This is an exquisite early bloom.

Small, vivid iris growing to 5 in., suitable for edging, or rockery. Try also in pots for January flowering.

Plant in swathes along paths, lawns. Free and long-flowering, a good carpet plant for bigger spring bulbs.

Spectacular late summer bulb. Will stay for years in sheltered, warm spot, 6 in. deep, rich loam.

Marble white blooms enliven faded late summer garden; plant in herbaceous border, among shrubs.

This, like other less hardy bulbs, needs winter protection (e.g. bracken). Unusual evergreen leaves.

July, Crinium powellii

August, Galtonia candicans

September, Zephyranthes

Bulbs are efficient plants since their cultivation is generally straightforward, many will spread unaided once established, and they bloom throughout the year indoors and out. Though initially dear to buy, they are an unrivalled investment for a colourful garden, so versatile they can be used everywhere, even in the restricted spaces of containers and bowls. Here are some less familiar bulbs.

April, Erythronium 'Pagoda'

May, Sparaxis

June, Allium ostrowskianum

Ornamental onions, usually trouble-free, spread easily, make good cut flowers. Need sunny position.

Lifted annually like gladiolus. Favoured, sunny, hot position required. Not easy, but worth trying.

Ideal to naturalize in shady and woodland areas: looks like a wild flower, fragrant, easy to grow.

Rivals better known autumn crocus with late season, brilliant yellow flowers, and later leaves. Light soil.

Looks delicate, but hardy and naturalizes. Decorative leaves, many flowers, scented. Best in woodland.

Showy, single or semi-double flowers, excellent for cutting, finely divided leaves. Rich soil, in border.

October, Sternbergia

November, Cyclamen cilicium

December, Poppy Anemone

The Everlasting Garden

Many flowers have everlasting features – their stems, leaves or seed heads often persist well after the plant itself has died; but some are so striking they are specially grown for indoor decoration.

Grasses: until recently, only a few grasses were grown widely for decorative purposes. The maize (1) is the largest. Buy a variety with multicoloured cobs. Grasses (2) should be sown in boxes and transplanted, otherwise they may be pulled up mistakenly for weeds.

Shrubs: we illustrate shrub rose gallica versicolor (3) which has attractive hips that last a long time. The enormous beige mops of the dead hydrangea flowers (4) last indefinitely indoors.

Large herbaceous plants: the foxglove, the hollyhock and so forth. Their tall spires will last a long time indoors. *Acanthus mollis* (5), bear's breeches, is a handsome plant whose statuesque flower heads look everlasting even when alive. The achilleas (6), yarrows, have flattish panicle heads composed of many flowers. The heads can be left or dyed. Some of the Erygiums (7), sea hollies, are large plants, others medium-sized. Their dried, prickly appearance is most distinctive.

Small herbaceous plants: Honesty (8) has already been lauded in Stage 13. Alchemillas (9), Lady's mantles, are a favourite of the indoor floral arranger. The limoniums (10), sea lavenders, known as statice, are frequently dyed, though there is a wide natural colour range. Nearly all the poppies (11) provide decorative seed heads. Catananche (14) should be planted in a sunny position.

Annuals: the helichysums (12) are the true everlasting flowers, which if cut just at full flower and hung head down to dry, will retain much of their original and various colours. Nigella (13), love-in-a-mist, is an example of an annual with bizarre dried seed heads. Moluccella (15), Irish bells, is related to the nettle. The whole plant can be cut and dried.

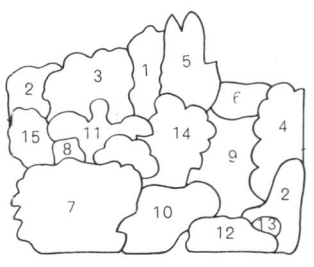

The Rose Garden

There is a sense of timelessness in the world of the rose. The rose garden can be lavish: there is no need here for hard geometry. Roses can ramble freely as ground cover, hummocky bushes, trailers, creepers, climbers and festooners. Out of bloom these older varieties have the character to make interesting shrubs. In bloom, they are more subtle and mysterious than so many modern roses. *Rosa wichuraiana* (1) borders the path. The old shrub roses are divided according to their origin and hybridization. For example, the 'cabbages' (centifolias) have open growth, large leaves, and globular flowers typical of old Dutch paintings: De Meaux (2). The 'chinas' are perpetual flowering, suitable for small gardens: Old Blush (3), the 'monthly' rose, is here treated as a hedge. The 'bourbons' have incomparable scent: Mme Isaac Pereire (4). The 'gallicas' have tiny bristles rather than prickles and make dense bushes: here in a tub is the spectacular crimson and white splashed flower of Rosa Mundi (5), Fair Rosamund. The 'mosses' have moss-like growth, often crimson, on the buds, and a long flowering period: Mutabilis (6). 'Hybrid perpetuals', developed from the old roses: Ferdinand Pichard (7). The 'musks' recall the modern floribundas: Buff Beauty (8). Polyantha grandiflora (9) is a climbing musk rose which festoons trees. The superb rugosa or 'ramanas' roses (Stage 4): Frau Dagmar Hastrup (10). Climbing roses include 'noisettes': Gloire de Dijon (11). Mermaid (12) is an example of a single flowered climber, which will reach 25 ft. Modern 'hybrid shrub' roses are post-1945 introductions, the quality of the rose has not been sacrificed to the size or shape of the flower: Nymphenburg (13), Schoolgirl (14). Use ground cover plants beneath and around the roses, suppressing the weeds and giving their own colour to the garden. Small plants such as Alyssum (16) or Forget-me-not (15), and bulbs such as scilla, chionodoxa, snowdrop, crocus, or winter aconite, are all a part of our rose garden.

The Perfumed Garden

The scents of most flowers are volatile oils, most fully appreciated in a sunny, wind-free corner as dusk falls and the fragrance wafts on the still, warm air – so a comfortable seat 1 is the first essential of a perfumed garden, preferably in an arbour of roses, 2 Zephirine Drouhin and honeysuckle, 3 *Lonicera japonica halliana*. 4 Surround your seat with heady smells by raising around it a 2–3 ft. elevated bed to lift scents closer to you and stock it with musky flowers – 5 nepeta, 6 stocks, 7 wallflowers, 8 sweet William, 9 nicotiniana, 10 Madonna lily, and 11 evening primrose, as well as aromatic herbs like 12 lavender and 13 rosemary. Herbs like 14 thyme and 15 pennyroyal (*Mentha*) give off their best bouquet when crushed, so set them along paths to be trodden on. Shrubs and trees that savour sweetly are 16 *Buddleia globosa*, 17 *Sambucus canadensis*, 18 *Viburnum fragrans*, 19 *Mahonia japonica*, 20 *Magnolia soulangeana* and 21 mock orange (*Philadelphus* 'Beauclerk'). 22 the rustling leaves and canes of the bamboo (*Arundinaria murieliae*), 23 Japanese wind chimes, 24 a tinkling fountain and pool and – above all – the contented humming and buzzing of bees and other insects drawn by the incense of the perfumed garden.

Preserve the perfume of your garden and refresh your home with lavender bags (cotton or muslin bags filled with lavender heads dried in the sun or airing cupboard) or with a simple pot pourri: dried wallflower petals mixed with dried rosemary sprigs and 30 grams of Orris root, and 1 tsp, nutmeg. Pot pourris are ancient preparations used to sweeten rooms, lightly scent clothes, and give freshness to linens, and pomanders contain the mixture. There are innumerable recipes, many closely guarded secrets, but flower petals are their principal base. Every mixture needs a fixative like Orris root which prolongs the life of the scents of these pot pourris.

The Herb Garden

Herb gardening has become popular again, and such is the variety and diversity of herbs that large garden areas can be devoted to the various groups of these plants – medicinal herbs, culinary herbs, scented herbs and so forth. Medicinal and culinary herbs should not be grown together unless they have first been properly identified. The Cottage/Perennial Garden and the Historical Garden, are examples of special gardens where many if not all the plants have some herbal characteristics. The herbs in illustration 1 were once very widely grown; some are still familiar today but others are seen infrequently. All are perennial, will spread naturally and, given a light, well-drained soil, are reasonably hardy. Mint (1), chives (2) and thyme (3) are probably the most widely-grown of all herbs – thyme usually as a flower. Hyssop (4) and horehound (5) make attractive edging plants, the former providing an excellent flavoured honey. Costmary (6) is rare. The more unusual herbs in this group have probably lost favour because their astringent taste is too strong for the modern palate. Sage (7) is an exception. Marjoram (8) is not the same as our wild plant. The herbs in illustration 2 are annuals and biennials – or herbs best treated as annuals. All are familiar in the kitchen and are widely used in Britain and America. Try growing them from seed, and use cloches for an early start in spring. Later you can make your own dill (9) vinegar for pickling, or sprinkle caraway (10) seeds over baked apples.

Parsley (11) is more or less a vegetable – two crops can be produced in one year. If your gardening space is restricted, try a pot of parsley. Chervil (12), although universally grown in France, is not common in Britain; parsley, chervil, tarragon (13) and chives make *fines herbes*. Borage (14) grows wild over much of Britain. Try aromatic basil (15). The other plants mentioned here belong to the herb groups but their former uses have waned; this is particularly true of the old medicinal plants. Both elecampane and mullein are wild plants, the latter with a tall spire of grey, woolly leaves and yellow flowers.

The Vegetable Garden

Vegetables do not have to be grown at the end of your garden out of sight; Many are decorative and can be bedded in patches among the ornamental plants. Long straight rows of one vegetable are more suited to large-scale growing than to small gardens; but set out in shapes such as circles and squares, vegetable gardens look like huge tapestries. Using vegetables in this way reduces insect damage and disease; there is danger of serious infestation when they are grown in large one-crop areas.

Three vital factors in vegetable growing are: soil fertility, rotation of crops and the timing of crops. Cropping takes plant foods out of the soil which must be replaced by manuring, fertilizing and conditioning. Rotation is also essential for families of vegetables have different requirements, take different nutrients out of the soil. Rotate crops around the brassicas (green vegetables), root vegetables and the legumes (peas and beans); grow beans after cabbages, or potatoes after peas. 'Catch cropping' is a technique to sow quick-maturing vegetables between rows of those slower growing.

In planning a vegetable patch, sowing and harvesting follow in sequences according to the types of vegetable and the season. Cold frames and cloches are indispensable, they extend the practicable growing season by weeks.

July (top left) Chives (sown April) divide the plot into four. Vegetable spaghetti (sown April, under glass) is a bright green, flask-shaped marrow, turning yellow when cooked, with insides like spaghetti. The climbing purple-podded French bean (sown April, under glass) has purple flowers and pods which turn green when cooked. Stake for climbing. Scorzonera (sown April) links this plot to the next. A black-rooted plant with sweet, white flesh,

it looks like the dandelion, and can be harvested during winter.
October (top right) The Black Spanish radish (sown July) divides the plot. Left in the ground until mid-winter, it can be lifted as required. Broad beans (sown fall) will over-winter to be harvested in late spring. They replace the Jamberry, an exotic 'tomato' (sown April, under glass). Endive (sown July) is a valuable winter salad. Blanch by tying the leaves together. Seakale beet (sown July) has leaves like spinach, and links this plot to the next.
January (below right) Jerusalem artichoke (tubers planted April) is harvested now, to be cooked in several ways. Around it the shallot (planted now) is harvested in midsummer. The purple-sprouting broccoli (sown April) will be harvested next April when vegetables are scarce. Leading to the next plot is flowering cabbage (sown April), harvested in winter.
April Golden beet (sown now) has flavourful flesh. Florence fennel (sown now, under glass) has aniseed flavour. Asparagus pea (sown now, under glass) has edible pods. Linking to next plot is ornamental kale (sown now, under glass). Even in quite a tiny backyard – even in a tiny city yard – it is possible to grow a surprisingly wide range of vegetables surprisingly well. Use raised beds (made from railway ties or planks) filled with growing mix. Space plants only half as far apart as most books tell you, but harvest them smaller. Really pack your plants in close together. Optimise on what you grow: use thinnings to flavour stews, broths, salads and so on. Don't segregate ornamentals from food plants: they're all plants together. Besides, many vegetables are highly decorative. Like runner beans, ornamental cabbages, purple broccoli and many others.

David Eaton

The Fruit Garden

As commercial fruit-growing concentrates more and more on the best marketable varieties, so your own garden becomes important for growing favourite fruits that are difficult, or expensive to buy. Horticulturists have responded by offering a new range of plants bred for the convenience of the small grower. The modern fruit garden is a movable mini-orchard, where bush fruits planted in gaily-coloured tubs on casters can be wheeled around the garden, where 'family' apple trees have several varieties on a plant to ensure pollination, and where gooseberries and other cane fruits are grown as vines on a trellis in the French manner. Fruits make excellent ornamental plants and today no garden is too small to try at least one kind of fruit.

Chinese gooseberry (Actinidia chinensis), above, an edible fruiting vine – highly attractive for its large heart-shaped leaves and long twining stems, is worth substituting for the clematis or climbing rose. Once established, it is vigorous and its white flowers produce strange bristly fruits rather like brown elongated pullet's eggs, tasting of gooseberry. You might find one in a big market, but why not plant your own in the sunniest part of your terrace and mulch well or store over winter indoors? Buy a good fruiting clone.

Boysenberry Both blackberry and raspberry are in its parentage; it will hold its own and bear fruit prolifically in a rough part of your garden, or used as a hedge, or as a thick screen for unsightly areas. The boysenberry fruits on the current season's canes and will bear for several years.

Peach, left. The 'container' plant for your garden or patio is the bush peach. Its globular shape is attractive at all times of the year. Once planted, it flowers and fruits even as soon as its second year; in those parts of the country where it is not reliably hardy, it can be moved to a sheltered winter location. Of Chinese origin, the peach has been cultivated for thousands of years, and the luscious quality of its fruit is symbolised as an adjective in our language. Try it, too, as an espalier (which is the traditional way) on a south or on a west wall.

The Seaside Garden

A large number of our inhabitants live on or near the sea. They have to cope with salt-laden gales, blown sand, and drought, but they can also learn how to exploit the absence of frosts. Wind is the common problem of all maritime situations. There are two lines of defence: first, the trees which withstand winds and form shelterbelts; second, the small trees and shrubs which form the hedges. **Trees** (shown along the coast in the background of our picture). Suitable species include: *Pinus radiata* (Monterey pine), *Pinus pinea* (stone pine), *Cupressus macrocarpa* (Monterey cypress), and *Quercus ilex* (holm oak), which are all evergreen. *Acer pseudoplatanus* (sycamore), *Populus alba* (white poplar), *Sorbus aria* (whitebeam): deciduous. **Hedges and shrubs.** The wattle fence in our illustration is put up as temporary cover until the shrubs are established. Behind it is *Hippophaë rhamnoides* (sea buckthorn), attractively grey-leaved and orange berried, but too invasive to go in the garden. In front is *Crataegus orientalis* (hawthorn), *Berberis gagnepainii* (barberry), and *Spartium junceum* (Spanish broom) – whose sheets of yellow flowers are outstanding in spring. Other hedging shrubs, here grown as specimens, include: *Olearia haastii* (daisy bush), *Escallonia macrantha* (escallonia) for milder areas, and fuchsia – definitely for mild areas. *Senecio greyi* (senecio) has soft grey leaves and bright yellow flowers, whereas *Griselinia littoralis* (griselina) has vivid green, glossy leaves. These two plants demonstrate a contrast in adaptation. **Other plants.** Kniphofia is an example of a herbaceous perennial which looks particularly appropriate in a seaside setting. Scotch thistle will grow eight foot from seed in two years. All sedums do well on the coast, as do spurges. *Euonymus fortunei radicans* (euonymus) is a vine to try. Also native seaside plants.

The Ecological Garden

When a butterfly or bird flies into town, it is not looking for a neat lawn and well-dug flower beds, but shelter (thick foliage) and food (insects, berries and nectar-rich flowers). You can offer both in a wild corner planted partly with stock from nurseries and seedsmen and partly with beautiful flowers that are too often dismissed as weeds. **1** Ornamental grasses can be grown cheaply from seed. (Ornamental wheat, *Triticum spelta*, is easy to rear.) The grass should *not* be left to run totally amok but should be cut at least once a year, in early September. **2** Plantains are invasive plants that spring up naturally on hard soil in wild corners. **3** A nesting box could have a perch for song birds while boulders set round the base will shelter toads and hedgehogs. **4** Butterflies can be supplied by butterfly farms. They will also tell you how to attract butterflies to your garden. **5** Hedgerow plants come in decorative species that are sold by most nurseries. **5** Hazel (*Corylus avellana*) gives a coppice effect. **6** Buddleia (*alternifolia* shown here) is one of the butterfly bushes. Here it has attracted some butterflies, the small tortoiseshells. **7** Eglantine (*Rosa rubiginosa*) is a strong hardy rose. **8** Bramble (*Rubus odoratus*) attracts bees as well as butterflies. It should be kept pruned and, like all these woodland shrubs, is *not* for small gardens. **9** Ivy (*Hedera helix*) and **10** Honeysuckle (*Lonicera periclymenum*) both play host to many insects. Wild flowers should *never* be dug up from their natural habitat. But all these can be bought and seed sown between September and April except in soggy, frosty or snowy conditions. The seeds, which may lie dormant for as long as a year or more, should be raked lightly into the soil surface. **11** Cowslip (*Primula veris*), **12** Birdsfoot trefoil (*Lotus corniculatus*), **13** Sweet Cicely or Myrrh (*Myrrnis odorata*), **14** Everlasting pea (*Lathyrus latifolius*), **15** Meadow cranesbill or wild geranium (*Geranium pratense*), **16** Comfrey (*Symphytum officinale*), and **17** Bouncing Bet or Soapwort (*Saponaria officinalis*) are all perennials. **18** Bluebell (*Hyacinthoides nonscripta*) is a bulb while **19** the Foxglove (*Digitalis purpurea*), **20** Wallflower (*Cheiranthus*), and **21** Sweet Rocket (*Hesperis matronalis* are biennial. On the Sweet Rocket here is resting a Cabbage White butterfly. Between them these plants and herbs all provide cover, nectar and food for bees, insects, butterflies, beetles and moths.

The Future Garden

Conserving energy resources is our slogan for the future. Solar energy and wind energy are two forms which are renewed all the time; future houses might have roofs with a device to absorb the sun's energy in some way and store it. A small domestic windmill might also be used. Some of our house's water supply might be recirculated. Rain-water tanks would provide all garden-irrigation supplies. In our illustration, the principal room of the house is a garden room, where indoors and outdoors meet, overcoming some of the vagaries of the weather. Along one boundary wall runs a leisure activities extension, not unlike a series of stables: it contains a hobbies room; a greenhouse and propagation room with artificial lighting; a dark house for growing mushrooms, and storing home-made wine. Constructed of modules, the householder can add or subtract the number of units or rooms he requires. The roof of the extension is a patio, lined with containers of soilless composts for herbs and young plants; behind are a vine-covered trellis and cut flowers for the house – grown in built-in planters. The garden below is devoted to fruits and vegetables, the mini-orchard of dwarf bush fruits lying in the middle-ground by a patch of lawn in the sunniest, most sheltered spot in the garden. Exciting new vegetables, like some of the recently introduced beans, are grown with the more traditional crops. Household refuse goes on compost on to the garden. Modern genetics allow a plantsman to produce a plant for a specific market in type, colour or form; yet we use our knowledge and skill in our own gardens to grow a particular variety which interests and pleases us. Scientists are placing more emphasis upon the importance of our gardens as repositories of plants which are no longer grown widely or on a commercial scale. Our 'wild garden', growing plants which attract wildlife (The Ecological Garden), is to the side of the house. Finally, there are rabbits, beehives, and doves.

Summary

In this part of the book we've tried to fire your imagination by shooting a whole host of ideas at you. Take any idea that really appeals to you and incorporate it in your garden, but don't just copy the idea out of the book – make it your own. Adapt it, modify it, add your own ideas to it, so that it becomes yours, because a garden is a highly personal thing, a projection of your own personality – so you don't want it simply to reflect someone else's personality.

But gardening does not end with the ideas you have seen in the second part of this book. There are more ideas about gardens and gardening than we've shown you here or than any book could show you. But if we have opened your mind to gardens, keep your eyes alert for other ideas: there are Japanese gardens, sand gardens, pebble gardens, peat gardens, bog gardens and a whole host of other types of gardens which we have not been able to show. You can see these for yourself: visit some of the great gardens in your locality. You'll find more ideas in most of these great gardens than you could use in your own garden.

It's worth remembering, though, when you look at the great gardens that they are, usually, very much larger than your garden, and that things that may look marvellous in the rolling acres of Kew or the Arnold Arboretum, could look ridiculous in your smaller garden. It's all a matter of scale. A huge cedar that looks magnificent spreading its branches across an ancient lawn in spacious surroundings, would probably fill the whole of your backyard and leave you no room to grow anything else, while a relatively small tree that would look just right in your garden would be lost in the ancestral acres of a country home. Thus it is not always easy simply to transpose an idea from one garden to another. Size, scale, perspective all need to be adjusted to fit your own needs.

Whatever you do in or with your garden, never let it become static: it probably won't let you let it anyway, because plants keep growing which changes the aspect of all the plants around it. Always give yourself enough to do to keep your interest and curiosity alive, but never so much to do it becomes a burden. Adopt that philosophy and you'll enjoy gardening for the rest of your life.

Bug Recognition Chart

Glossary of Gardening Terms

Annual = a plant which grows from seed to flower and sets seed and dies in one season

Biennial = a plant which makes growth in its first year, flowers, seeds and dies in its second season

Broadcast = the scattering of seed at random on a prepared bed

Dibber or dibbler = a wooden or sometimes steel-tipped tool used for making holes in seed beds for the sowing of individual seeds or the setting out of small transplants

Drill = a narrow, shallow V-shaped trench in the soil into which seed is sown

Fungicides = fungus preventives or curatives

Herbicides = weedkillers

Humus = decayed vegetable matter which, mixed with the soil, is essential to healthy plant growth

Hybrid = a deliberate cross between two similar plants to produce a third, intermediate but superior plant

Insecticides = substances which kill insects but not other bugs

Perennial = any plant which continues to grow, year after year. Herbaceous perennials die to ground level each winter

Pesticides = pest killers

Propagation = the deliberate increase of horticultural plants

Pruning = the removal of branches or buds in order to promote the growth of healthy and productive wood

Spit = the depth of a spade. Double-digging = digging to twice the depth of a spade

Transplant = a young plant grown from seed and ready to be planted out

Vines = a term now widely used for all climbing plants

Glossary of Latin and Common Names

African lily = *Agapanthus praecox*
African marigold = *Tagetes erecta*
African violets = *Saintpaulia* forms
Agapanthus praecox = Blue Nile or African lily
Allium cepa = onion
Amelanchier laevi grandiflora = snowy mespilus
Apium graveolens = celery
Apricot = *Prunus armeniaca*
Aubergine = *Solanum melongena*
Aubretia = *Aubrieta deltoides*
Aubrietia deltoides = aubretia
Autumn crocus = *Crocus sativus*

Beans, English broad or fava = *Vicia faba*
Beans, snap, kidney or dwarf French = *Phaseolus vulgaris*
Beets = *Beta vulgaris*
Berberis thunbergii = common berberis
Beta vulgaris = beets
Blue Nile lily = *Agapanthus praecox*

Cabbage = *Brassica oleracea* var. *capitata*
Calendula officinalis = English or pot marigold
California hyacinth = *Galtonia candicans*
Canary climber = *Tropaeolum peregrinum*
Candytuft = *Iberis umbellata*
Carrots = *Daucus carota*
Celery = *Apium graveolens*
Chaenomeles 'Rowallane' = flowering quince
Cheiranthus cheiri = wallflower

Christmas rose = *Helleborus niger*
Climbing hydrangea = *Hydrangea petiolaris*
Colchicum = *Colchicum autumnale*
Colchicum autumnale = Colchicum
Common berberis = *Berberis thunbergii*
Common cotoneaster = *Cotoneaster simonsii*
Common mahonia = *Mahonia aquifolium*
Corn = *Zea mays*
Cotoneaster horizontalis = herringbone cotoneaster
Cotoneaster simonsii = common cotoneaster
Crinum x powellii = Paradise lily
Crocus sativus = autumn crocus
Cucurbita mixta = pumpkin
Cucurbita spp = marrows/squashes
Cyclamen (houseplant types) = *Cyclamen persicum* strains
Cyclamen persicum strains = houseplant cyclamen
Cydonia sp. = *Chaenomeles* sp.

Daffodil = *Narcissus* spp.
Dahlia = *Dahlia hybrida*
Dahlia hybrida = Dahlia
Daucus carota = carrot
Dwarf wayfaring tree = *Viburnum opulus* 'Compactus'
Dwarf winter iris = *Iris danfordiae*

Eggplant/aubergine = *Solanum melongena*
English marigold = *Calendula officinalis*

Flowering quince = *Chaenomeles* forms
French marigold = *Tagetes patula*

Galtonia candicans = California hyacinth
Geranium (red) = *Pelargonium zonale*
Grape vine = *Vitis vinifera*

Harlequin flower = *Sparaxis hybrida*
Helianthus annuus = sunflower
Helleborus niger = Christmas rose
Herringbone cotoneaster = *Cotoneaster horizontalis*
Honesty = *Lunaria biennis*
Humulus japonicus 'Variegatus' = ornamental hop
Hyacinths = *Hyacinthus orientalis* forms
Hyacinthus orientalis = hyacinth
Hydrangea petiolaris = climbing hydrangea
Hypericum patulum = St. John's wort

Iberis umbellata = candytuft
Ice plant = *Sedum spectabile*
Ipheion uniflorum = spring star flower
Iris danfordiae = dwarf winter iris

Japonica = *Chaenomeles* spp.

Kniphofia uvaria = Torch lily or red-hot poker

Lactuca sativa = Lettuce

Lathyrus odoratus = sweet pea
Lavender = *Lavandula spicata*
Lavandula spicata = lavender
Lettuce = *Lactuca sativa*
Lilac = *Syringa vulgaris*
Lunaria biennis = honesty
Lycopersicum esculentum = tomato

Mahonia aquifolium = common mahonia
Malus x 'Golden Hornet' = yellow-fruiting crab
Marrows = *Cucurbita* spp
Mock orange = *Philadelphus* spp
Mountain ash = *Sorbus aucuparia*

Narcissus hybrids = daffodils
Nasturtium = *Tropaeolum major*
Tropaeolum peregrinum = Canary climber
Tropaeolum major = nasturtium
Nectarine = *Prunus persica* form

Onion = *Allium cepa*
Ornamental hop = *Humulus japonicus* 'Variegatus'

Papaver rhoeas hybrids = Shirley poppies
Paradise lily = *Crinum x powellii*
Peach = *Prunus persica*
Pear = *Pyrus communis* forms
Peas, English, snow or sugar = *Pisum sativum*
Peas, snow = *Pisum sativum*
Peas, sugar = *Pisum sativum*
Pelargonium zonale = geranium (red)
Periwinkle = *Vinca minor*

Petunia = *Petunia* hybrid strains
Phaseolus coccineus = scarlet runner bean
Phaseolus vulgaris = beans, snap, kidney or dwarf French
Philadelphus spp = syringa or mock orange
Potato = *Solanum tuberosum*
Pot marigold = *Calendula officinalis*
Prunus armeniaca = apricot
Prunus persica forms = peach, nectarine
Pyrus communis = pear
Pumpkins = *Cucurbita mixta*

Radish = *Raphanus sativus*
Raphanus sativus = radish
Red-hot poker = *Kniphofia uvaria*
Rose = *Rosa* species and named forms
Rowan = *Sorbus aucuparia*

Saintpaulia = *Saintpaulia* forms
Saintpaulia forms = Saintpaulia/African violets
Scarlet runner bean = *Phaseolus coccineus*
Shirley poppy = *Papaver rhoeas* hybrids
Snowy mespilus = *Amelanchier grandiflora*
Solanum melongena = eggplant/aubergine
Solanum tuberosum = potato
Sorbus aucuparia = mountain ash/rowan
Spring star flower = *Ipheion uniflorum*

Sparaxis hybrida = Harlequin flower
Spinacea oleracea = spinach
Spinach = *Spinacea oleracea*
Squashes = *Cucurbita* spp
Sternbergia = *Sternbergia lutea*
Sternbergia lutea = Sternbergia
St. John's wort = *Hypericum patulum*
Sunflower = *Helianthus annuus*
Sweet peas = *Lathyrus odoratus*
Syringa = *Philadelphus* spp
Syringa vulgaris = lilac

Tagetes erecta = African marigold
Tagetes patula = French marigold
Thyme = *Thymus vulgaris*
Thymus vulgaris = thyme
Tomato = *Lycopersicum esculentum*
Torch lily = *Kniphofia uvaria*
Tulipa hybrids = tulips
Tulips = *Tulipa* hybrids

Viburnum opulus 'Compactum' = dwarf wayfaring tree
Vicia faba = beans, English broad or fava
Vinca minor = periwinkle
Vitis vinifera = grape vine

Wallflower = *Cheiranthus cheiri*

Yellow-fruiting crab = *Malus x* 'Golden Hornet'

Zea mays = corn

Index

Acer pseudoplatanus (sycamore) 130
African violets 75
Ajuga reptans (bugle) 109
Annual bed 29
Annuals 38, 45
Ants 38
Asplenium nidus-avis (bird's nest fern) 115
Azaleas 67

Bacteria 81
Barberry (*Berberis gagnepainii*) 130
Barrel-tubs 100
Beans
  bush snap 41, 44
  dwarf French 41, 44
  pole 27, 41
  scarlet runner 26
Bedding plants 38
Bees 46
Beetles 58
Berberis gagnepainii 130
Berberis thunbergii 67
Biennials 45
Bin, compost 26
Birdsfoot trefoil (*Lotus corniculatus*) 133
Bird's nest fern (*Asplenium nidus-avis*) 115
Blackfly 30
Bluebell (*Hyacinthoides nonscripta*) 59, 133
Bonemeal 29, 64
Bordeaux mixture 81
Border, pre-sown 31
Bottle, garden 96, 113
Bramble (*Rubus odoratus*) 133
Buddleia 133
Bug hunting 69
Bulbs 74, 75, 117
  planting 59

Cacti bowl 96
Caddis fly 66
Calendula 29, 50
Camellias 67
Campanula carpatica 106
Canary climber 37
Carex morrowii 109
Casts, worm 62
Caterpillars 42
Cats 48
Centipedes 38
Chaenomeles 'Rowallane' 67

Cheiranthus (wallflower) 133
Chemicals 42
Chionodoxa 59
Chives 125
Christmas rose (*Helleborus niger*) 68
Chrysanthemums 35, 66
Cissus antarctica (kangaroo vine) 115
Clay soil 49
Clematis 106
Cloches 81
Colchicums 48, 49
Comfrey (*Symphytum officinale*) 133
Compost
  aeration 78
  temperature 34
Compost activator 34
Compost bin 26
Conditioner, soil 70
Conservatory 115
Container-grown plants 68
Container planting 71
Costmary 125
Cotoneaster dammeri 106
  horizontalis 106
  simonsii 65
Courgettes 33
Cowslip (*Primula veris*) 133
Crateagus orientalis (hawthorn) 130
Creeping Jenny (*Lysimachia nummularia*) 109
Crocus 59
Croton hybrid (Joseph's coat) 115
Cupressus macrocarpa (Monterey cypress) 130
Cuttings 75, 79
Cyclamen 72

Daffodils 58, 62
Dahlias 42, 66
Daisy bush (*Olearia haastii*) 130
Damp bed, making a 109
Derris 69
Dibbler 29
Dig, how to 27
Digitalis purpurea (foxglove) 133
Division 79
Dogs 48
Dracaena 100

Earwigs 46
Eglantine (*Rosa rubiginosa*) 133
Escallonia (*Escallonia macrantha*) 130

Euonymus (*Euonymus fortunei radicans*) 130
Everlasting pea (*Lathyrus latifolius*) 133

Farmyard manure 64
Ferns 75
Fertilizers 64
  artificial 70
Ficus benjamina (weeping fig) 115
Fish meal 70
Fittonia verschaffeltii (snakeskin plant) 115
Fluorescent light tubes 113
Foliar feeds 65
Fountain 83
Foxglove (*Digitalis purpurea*) 133
Frames 81
Front garden 83
Frost 62
Fruit trees 65
Fungus diseases 81
Furniture, garden 83

Gardener's garters (*Phalaris arundinacea* 'Picta') 109
Geranium endressii 106
Geranium pratense (meadow cranesbill) 133
Gladiolus 43
Grafting 79
Grape ivy (*Rhoicissus rhomboidea*) 115
Grass seeding 49
Greenfly 30
Greenhouse 83
Griselinia (*Griselinia littoralis*) 130

Hanging basket 83
Hardwood cuttings 79
Hazel (*Corylus avellana*) 133
Heathers 75, 106
Hedera Heisse (Heisse's ivy) 115
Hedera helix 133
Hedgehogs 48
Hedging 104
Helianthus annus 32
Helleborus niger (Christmas rose) 68
Herbaceous border 35
  perennials 69
Herbicides 32, 73
Herbs 78, 124
Hesperis matronalis (sweet rocket) 133
Hippophaë rhamnoides (sea buckthorn) 130

Holcus mollis 'Variegatus' 109
Holm oak (*Quercus ilex*) 130
Honesty (*Lunaria biennis*) 50
Honeysuckle (*Lonicera periclymenum*) 133
Horehound 125
Hormone rooting powder 79
Hosta crispula 109
House plants 75
Humulus japonicus 'Variegatus' 36
Hyacinthoides nonscripta (bluebell) 133
Hyacinths 58
Hydrangea petiolaris 82
Hygiene, garden 81
Hypericum calycinum 106
Hypericum patulum 66
Hyssop 125

Ice plant (*Sedum spectabile*) 75, 76
Ichneumon fly 66
Indoor plants 73, 113
Ipheion uniflora (star flower) 70
Irrigation, automatic 113
Ivies 75
Ivy (*Hedera helix*) 133

Jasminum nudiflorum (winter jasmine) 106
Joseph's coat (*Croton* hybrid) 115
Juniperus horizontalis var. *glauca* 106

Kangaroo vine (*Cissus antarctica*) 115
Korean chrysanthemum 69

Lamium galeobdolon 'Variegatum' 106
Lamium maculatum 106
Lathyrus latifolius (everlasting pea) 133
Lavender 62
Lawn
    edging 45
    fertilizer 64
    repairing 43
    shaping 41
Layering 79
Lime 70
Liquid feed 44, 64, 70
London pride (*Saxifraga umbrosa*) 109
Lotus corniculatus (birdsfoot trefoil) 133
Lysimachia nummularia (creeping Jenny) 109

Mahonia aquifolium 67
Malus 'Golden Hornet' 40

Manure, farmyard 64
Marrows, 33, 48
Maze 104
Meadow cranesbill (*Geranium pratense*) 133
Mint 125
Moisture meter 113
Monterey cypress (*Cupressus macrocarpa*) 130
Monterey pine (*Pinus radiata*) 130
Mountain ash (*Sorbus aucuparia*) 83
Myrrh (*Myrrhis odorata*) 133

Nasturtium 37

Olearia haastii (daisy bush) 130
Ornamental hop 36
Ornaments, garden 94

Patio 37, 39
Paving materials 39, 98
Pear trees 64
Peat 40, 64, 65
Pelargonium 38, 75
Perennials 45, 69
Pergola 83
Periwinkle 46, 47
Petunia 34
Phalaris arundinacea 'Picta' (Gardener's garters) 109
Phaseolus coccineus 26
Pinus pinea (stone pine) 130
Pinus radiata (Monterey pine) 130
Plant, how to 27
Plants
    indoor 73, 113
    recognizing types of 45
Polygonum aubertii (Russian vine) 106
Poppy 29
Populus alba (white poplar) 130
Primula veris (cowslip) 133
Propagation 79
Pruning 77
Pumpkins 33
Pyrethrum 69

Quercus ilex (holm oak) 130

Rake, lawn 80
Rhoicissus rhomboidea (grape ivy) 115
Ring culture 31
Rockery 67, 74, 75
Rosa paulii 106

Rosa rubiginosa (Eglantine) 133
Roses 60, 120
Rubus odoratus (bramble) 133
Russian vine (*Polygonum aubertii*) 106

Saponaria officinalis (soapwort) 133
Saxifraga umbrosa (London pride) 109
Scarlet runner 26
Sea buckthorn (*Hippophaë rhamnoides*) 130
Seaside gardening 130
Seaweed 65
Sedum spectabile (ice plant) 75, 76
Seed
    collection 59
    sowing 59
Senecio (*Senecio greyi*) 130
Sewer sludge 65
Sexual propagation 79
Shirley poppy 28, 101
Shoddy 65
Shrubs 67
Slugs 36, 81
Snails 36
Snakeskin plant (*Fittonia verschaffeltii*) 115
Snowdrop 59
Soapwort (*Saponaria officinalis*) 133
Softwood cuttings 79
Soil
    analysis 63
    improving 65
Soilless mixes 27, 65
Sorbus aria (whitebeam) 130
Sorbus aucuparia (mountain ash) 83
Spanish broom (*Spartium junceum*) 130
Spider plant 75
Squashes 33
Star flower (*Ipheion uniflora*) 70
Sticks, as markers 28
Stone pine (*Pinus pinea*) 130
Sunflower 32, 33
Sweet peas 80
Sweet rocket (*Hesperis matronalis*) 133
Sycamore (*Acer pseudoplatanus*) 130
Symphytum officinale (comfrey) 133

Terracotta strawberry pots 96
Thyme 125
Toad 44
Tomatoes 30, 31
Top-dressing 70

Topiary 104
Tradescantia 75
Tree-house 104
Trees
    fruit 65
    planting 51
    preparing ground for 47
Trellis 61
Triticum spelta (ornamental wheat) 133
Troughs 96

Vegetables 41, 126, 127
    harvesting 60
Vegetative propagation 79
Viburnum opulus 'Compactum' 67
Viburnum tomentosum 106
Vines 31
    planting 61

Virginia creeper 106

Walled garden 104
Wallflower (*Cheiranthus*) 44, 133
Washing-up liquid 30
Water, as bug deterrent 69
Weedkillers 32
Weeds 32, 42
Weeping fig (*Ficus benjamina*) 115
White poplar (*Populus alba*) 130
Window box 83
Winter jasmine (*Jasminum nudiflorum*)
  106
Worms 42
    casts of 62

Zebrina 75